GORAN POWELL

Waking Dragons

a martial artist faces his ultimate test

Foreword by GEOFF THOMPSON

summersdale

WAKING DRAGONS

Summersdale Publishers Ltd
46 West Street
Chichester
West Sussex
PO19 1RP
UK

www.summersdale.com

Printed and bound in Great Britain

ISBN: 1-84024-513-1
ISBN: 978-1-84024-513-4

Contents

Foreword...5

Glossary..7

The Field of Truth..9

The Rainbow Club...15

London Calling..22

First Contact..26

Spanish Lessons..43

Beer and Schnapps...52

The Knockdown...66

The Pit of Despair...80

The Knockout...89

The Wilderness Months.................................104

Curtain Road...113

Sensei, Sempai...142

Shihan, Hanshi...154

Testing Grounds...162

Ups and Downs..171

Dark Clouds..178

Park Life..186

Heavy Bag...196

Hard Sparring...201

Waking Dragons...206

Aftermath..225

Epilogue..235

Afterword..236

Acknowledgements..238

Education of a Martial Artist..........................240

To my Senseis, Joe Claronino, Stav, Chris Rowen and Gavin Mulholland; and to my first Sempai, the late Gary Malcolm. Thank you for teaching me.

Foreword

It is rare that I get a book landing on my doorstep that actually has something new, something substantial to say about karate and the combat arts. Most manuscripts I read are so busy taking themselves way too seriously that I don't usually manage to get past the introduction. This wonderful book by Goran Powell does not, I am delighted to say, fall into this category; rather it falls into that rare category of books that leave you inspired and wanting more. What I love about this book (apart from the fact that it is written beautifully – rare in a martial arts book) is the fact that it is about me. And it is about you. It is about all of us. Don't be fooled by the title of the book – this is about much more than match-fighting 30 fresh opponents, this is much more than looking into the belly of karate; this book is about facing the inner opponent, it is about looking into the belly of fear itself. As a species, we have an innate urge to stretch the boundaries of our world by stepping into discomfort, and from my experience so far on this spinning planet discomfort is where all the action is. All the gold is neatly stacked in great abundance just behind the wall of fear that most of us dare not even attempt to surmount. So this book is great because it is less about karate and more about human nature, it is great because it is less about the Thirty Man Kumite and more about challenging our limitations and growing a little cerebral muscle. It is not about belts and badges and trophies and awards. When you face 30 fresh opponents – one after the other, each trying to flatten the world with your head – it is about pure survival, about what you've got and who you are, and how each of you will react under extreme pressure. It is about cranking yourself up to your limit, taking a deep breath and then cranking it up some more.

This motivational book follows one man's brave journey to his own outer limits, and Goran's account will inspire you to leave the couch and take your own journey. Whatever and wherever that might be.

It inspired me, and I know it will inspire you.

Geoff Thompson

Glossary

Aikido	Flowing Japanese grappling art
Bunkai	Self-defence techniques
Dan	Levels of black belt
Dojo	Training hall
Escrima	Filipino martial art
Gi	Martial arts training suit
Goju Ryu	Okinawan style of karate
Hajime	Begin
Jujitsu	Japanese grappling art
Kata	Prearranged sequence of movements
Kyokushinkai	Full-contact style of karate
Ryu	Association
Sempai	Class senior or assistant instructor
Sensei	Instructor
Shotokan	Japanese style of karate
Taekwondo	Korean martial art
Tao	A tricky one to define, since the opening of the Taoist bible tells us *'that which can be expressed in words is not the eternal Tao'*. I use it playfully in the sense of *fate* or *that which life throws at you*.
Yame	Stop
Zen	Japanese Buddhism

The Field of Truth

It's one of those perfect English summer days: hazy sunshine, lush green trees and soft grass underfoot. We're gathered in a scouts' camp in the glorious countryside outside Portishead, just south of Bristol. In any other circumstances, we'd be kicking back and relaxing, throwing a frisbee or cracking open a few beers. But there's work to be done, and it isn't tying knots or collecting firewood. This is a karate camp.

The instructors have told everyone to meet on the small field near the entrance. They have taken to calling it the Field of Truth. They have a mean sense of humour.

No one knows why we're here, except Carl and me. I was told in confidence several weeks ago, and I managed to keep my mouth shut, which wasn't easy. Carl's been thinking of little else for the past few weeks. Or more likely months. He's about to attempt the Thirty Man Kumite.

He'll fight 30 people, one after another. They'll be the highest ranked fighters in our association. Every fight will be 'full contact'. It will last one minute. No gloves. No shin pads. No headguards. Full-power punches to the body are allowed, plus sweeps, throws, and kicks to the legs, body and head. No face punching. No strikes to the joints or groin. Carl will get a two-minute break after ten fights and another one after 20. If he's knocked out, or knocked down and can't continue, he will fail his test.

There's a small huddle of spectators on the Field of Truth. They are looking on curiously as 30 fighters line up along the far side of the field. Carl is warming up in the middle, alone with his thoughts, steeling himself for what lies ahead.

Nobody really knows what to expect. Many fighters in the line-up have not met Carl before. He's been away for a while. To the uninitiated, it looks like a massacre is about to occur. But I'm not so sure. I know Carl from the old days. I remember him winning medals at knockdown tournaments (heavyweight division). I remember him training with the British squad. I know what he's capable of with his kicks. As I take my place at the head of the line-up, I'm glad he'll be fighting 29 people before me.

The instructors call the proceedings to order. There's no great ceremony. We take a simple bow and the first fighter is called out. They begin. After a few seconds, Carl catches him with a head kick. It's perfectly controlled, because this is a grading, not a tournament. If it had been a tournament, the guy would be out cold. Instead, he collapses to his knees, badly dazed. After a short break the instructors get him on his feet, but for the rest of the fight, he stays well away from Carl.

The second fighter comes up and is promptly knocked down too. A pattern is beginning to form, and the line-up doesn't like what it's seeing.

Carl is making it look very easy to take someone's head off. Some of the less experienced fighters are starting to look decidedly nervous, wishing they were back in their tents, or better still, back home with the Sunday papers like every other normal human being.

Carl's plan is working nicely for him, and I begin to wonder whether he'll be troubled at all during his line-up. But even the best-laid plans can go astray.

Carl has already been training hard for two days, and the afternoon heat is intense. The sweating is causing his body to lose salt, which can bring on cramps. As early as the third fight, he begins to clutch at his hamstrings in pain. It looks like he's pulled a muscle.

The instructors stop the fight for a few seconds and give him the chance to stretch his legs. Then he's forced to continue. Meanwhile, the fighters in the line-up are taking no chances. They're badly spooked by what they saw earlier, and they're all going in hard to avoid getting picked off. This is bad news for Carl, and his real test is just beginning.

Kicking high is too painful now, so he's forced to trade punches and low kicks instead. By the time he reaches his first break, after ten fights, he's looking tired and dazed. He sits in the shade of tree, sipping water and stretching his hamstrings, trying to get them back into play.

It's no use. As the fighting begins again, it's clear he's going to have to do things the hard way... toe-to-toe. Soon he's struck by cramps again, and things begin to look ominous.

The instructors call a halt. They lay him on his front and massage the backs of his legs. He gets up, slowly, painfully, and forces himself to continue. As each fight goes on, he is climbing up the grades, facing stronger and stronger fighters. They're still mindful of his opening performance, and going in very hard.

The sun beats down on him unmercifully, and the tiredness is taking its toll, but the crowd refused to let him stop, or even slow down. They urge him on, shouting and screaming at him to hit back, throw punches and low kicks, to fight harder.

After 20 fights, Carl gets another short break. He takes some more water and stretches out his legs. Then the fighting begins again. Pretty soon, Carl is in a seriously bad way. Cramps strike him again and this time, he seems genuinely unable to continue. I watch as he sits forlornly in the shade of a tree, sipping water and massaging his legs. The instructors are clearly concerned, and talk to him quietly. For a moment, no one's quite sure what to do. They can't allow him a long break now. It would negate the test.

I begin to wonder if they are going to pull him out? Sensei Gavin is kneeling beside him. He looks around, scanning the horizon, as if searching for a solution. There isn't one. After a few seconds, he simply stands up and calls out the next fighter. There's a moment of stillness. Then Carl gets to his feet, in a trance, and squares up. The fighting resumes and he continues his battles through gritted teeth.

Now he is among the strongest, most powerful black belts. They put him under incredible pressure. One after another smashes away at his body and legs, dropping their body weight onto his battered thighs with the hard bones of their shins. There are no pads. This is just muscle and bone. Carl refuses to give in to the pressure, and hits back, but each new fighter is fresh, while Carl is at the edge of exhaustion.

He is close to the end of the line-up, and things are getting ugly. Mark launches a blistering attack on Carl, stalking him and then smashing away at his body and legs with massive, lightning-fast combinations. Steve smashes Carl's chest and ribs with huge, thudding punches and then switches to low kicks on the legs. Carl is taking massive punishment, but refuses to go down. His pride will not allow him to give in. He hits back as best he can.

Eventually his spirit takes him through 29 full-contact bouts. It is time for one final fight. I jog out to face him. He looked tired and shaken and I know his left leg is badly damaged. It has taken a terrible battering. Now, some people are cruel, and they would target this leg unmercifully, but I like to consider myself a gentleman, and prefer to attack other areas – the places that can still take a bit more punishment.

The fight begins and I test Carl with a few body shots. He wobbles slightly and throws a couple of slow punches. I avoid them easily and slam a couple of low kicks onto his 'good' leg. I can pick him off at will. I don't really want to knock him over on his last fight, but equally, I don't want it to be too easy. After all, this is his grand finale.

Suddenly, the same fact seems to register with Carl. It's his last fight. He shouts loudly, to encourage himself, and surges forward, throwing hard punches. He's summoning every last drop of energy. I notice the change immediately, and get up on my toes to avoid getting caught. Now we are fighting.

He throws a thunderous left, right combination. I back away to avoid the shots and ram a hard front kick into his gut. I hear a loud thud, and feel the air go out of him, but he's hyped up now and keeps coming.

He leans forward and grabs my shoulders, hoping to pull me onto a knee strike. Oi, Carl, man, I wasn't born yesterday! Before he can smash me, I hook a big right uppercut into his belly, just where the kick landed moments earlier. Nothing. Carl is unstoppable now. The crowd is yelling furiously, willing him on for one last, tremendous effort.

We trade punches and kicks, and Carl fights hard for one last, furious minute. Then it's all over. The timekeeper shouts 'Time!' and the instructors call 'Stop!' but we don't hear a thing. In the end, they step between us and wave their arms. We break.

Carl has done it. He's the first student in our association to complete the Thirty Man Kumite. Everyone is in awe of his achievement. No one has ever seen anything quite like it.

That evening we go to the local swimming baths, and Carl comes along to relax his tired muscles. His body is battered and bruised all over, but he's in good spirits. Some of the guys goof around in the pool. Carl relaxes in the hot tub, chatting to some of the younger members, basking in the glory of what he'd done earlier in the day.

Later, back at the camp, we prepare our evening meals over a kerosene stove. Carl's tent is pitched next to mine and Sensei Gavin's and Sensei Dan's. After eating his pasta, he tells us he's going to lie down 'just for half an hour'. He assures us he'll meet us later by the campfire.

We didn't see him again until late the next morning, and who could blame him?

The Rainbow Club

It's another wet Saturday morning. We're on an endless grey motorway, somewhere south of Birmingham. I'm sitting in the front seat, next to my dad, in our lilac Morris Marina estate, British Leyland's finest. We're going to a judo grading.

I can't recall where exactly, some place in Birmingham, or perhaps it was Wolverhampton? We were always driving up there, to Aston or Halesowen, to some judo tournament or other.

Every time was the same. The same empty feeling in the pit of my stomach, the cold sweats, the frequent toilet stops, the dry throat; and the same question, over and over again: *What am I doing here?* Why am I not back home in warm, gentle Worcester, playing happily in the street with all the other children?

We're looking for the Renbukan Judo Club. As usual, the directions we have are crap, so we stop to ask an old lady. 'There's no Rainbow Club around here darling,' she informs me. 'There is a bingo club…'

We keep searching until we find the mighty Renbukan. It's a little church hall, with no sign outside. There's nothing to indicate there might be judo inside. But as I go through the door the familiar smell of judo hits me: the damp, dusty, sweet, stale smell of a mat where hundreds of bodies have fought over the years.

I report to the instructors. They tick my name on their list and I get changed in a dingy little room. I wait, nervously. Eventually, I'm called up and demonstrate my throws. I have some fights and do some grappling on the ground. In the end, I pass my grading and get a new belt. I go home, pleased as punch.

That was how it always worked. Once the test was over, and the fighting done, I was delighted with myself, and very glad I'd done it.

My interest in judo began in 1972, when I was seven. Mum showed me a clipping from the Worcester Evening News. It was about a new sport called judo, where even the smallest person can throw the biggest person, once they know the secrets. She was quite fascinated by the martial arts, although she had no intention of trying them herself. She encouraged me to have a go. Dad offered to take me along to the club. It sounded magical. I agreed to give it a try.

On Saturday we drove along the Newtown Road and down Tallow Hill to St Paul's Judo Club in the city centre. Inside there was a large area of hard matting, covered in thick, dirty white canvas. Those were the days before those fancy green nylon mats were invented. The surface was as hard as nails, especially in winter. The only consolation was that as a kid, you didn't have far to fall.

I met the instructor, a small, kindly man called Jeff Woods. He wore a thick white canvas suit and an orange belt, and he had bad teeth. He wrote my name down on a scrap of paper.

'Goran,' I told him.

'*Gareth?*'

'Goran.'

'*Darren?*'

'G O R A N!!'

'Oh, *Gordon!* Why didn't you say?'

He showed me how to place my hands for a forward roll, fingers pointing back, to avoid hurting them as I went over. These were called breakfalls. I saw the other children running and tumbling across the mat, but I practised slowly a few more times. Then I learned a simple hip throw. We did a few exercises and I went home quite happy. It seemed fun.

I trained twice a week and was soon tumbling happily with the other kids, playing games and learning as we went along. Soon we were fighting for points, using throws, and hold-down. Later we learned arm-locks and strangles.

Jeff would call me out to fight: '*Darren! Gareth! Gordon!*' After many years together, we settled on *Garron*. Life has been much easier since Goran Ivanisevich won Wimbledon.

I would wrestle with one of my clubmates for a minute or two, and then someone else would come out and have a go. I didn't like being called out to fight, but once it started, I was fine. I won as often as I lost.

Often I would fight Jeff's son Greg, who was about my age. We got to know each other's style so well, neither could get anything on the other. Our matches always ended in a draw.

The club was run on a shoestring budget, and the roof had a habit of leaking. We would be rolling around, trying for a hold-down, with rainwater pouring onto the mat beside us. We were too busy fighting to take much notice.

A few years later, a karate class began to share our training hall. I would watch them training. They would stand in neat rows, punching the air and shouting. My dad had done a bit of boxing and he was unimpressed. 'They're just punching the air,' he'd mutter disdainfully. I had to admit, it looked a lot easier than judo. Judo was always a struggle.

Doing judo earned me a certain respect at school. The bullies tended to leave me alone and go in search of weaker prey. I enjoyed this freedom from oppression.

But after a few years, the fun began to go out of my training. We were getting bigger and older. The fights were getting tougher. I wanted to stay home or play with my mates in the street. My parents gently encouraged me not to give up.

Jeff wanted me to fight in the club team, so I began going up to tournaments in the Birmingham area. Because of my physique (Mum assured me I was *sturdy*, not fat) I always found myself in the heavier weight categories, fighting older boys. I rarely did well. Then one year, there was a new tournament based on age. This time, being the biggest and most experienced, I won a gold medal. I was the West Midlands judo champion.

I was over the moon. The West Midlands was practically the whole world as far as I was concerned. For a while it reignited my interest. I competed for two more years, winning more medals. But by the time I reached my teens, my interest was beginning to seriously wane.

It was around this time that the skateboard craze hit town. Every kid in the neighbourhood took their roller-skates apart and nailed them to a plank of wood. We were radical. I didn't want to spend my Saturday afternoons fighting on a smelly old mat. I wanted to do kick-flips, 360s and get airborne like Tony Alva or Stacey Peralta.

I saved up and bought a set of Kryptonic wheels (big reds if you must know, 70mm) and a set of Tracker trucks. Dad and I made decks out of fibreglass and wood, and we stuck sandpaper on top for extra grip. The kids built a ramp in the street and we went up and down, all day and late into the evening. Mum always made me come in before the other children. *Oh, Mum, just five more minutes, please!*

Next I bought an electric guitar and amplifier, and practised to be a rock star. I learned to play my favourite songs by Elvis Costello, Stiff Little Fingers and the Undertones. Finally at the age of 15, I put my foot down and told my parents I wasn't doing judo any more. They were saddened, but I was old enough to make my own decisions.

I decided to play basketball instead. I practised every day, but I never made it onto the school team. Sadly, there was only one team that I managed to get on, the one nobody wanted to get on: the cross-country team. It was my own fault. One of my teachers decided he'd had enough of my lip and told me to report to him after school. He ran the school cross-country team, and before I knew it, I was slogging along a muddy canal bank with a stitch in my side.

Actually, I didn't mind the running. It was hard, but not as hard as judo. Nothing was as hard as judo. When you're running, what's the worst that can happen? You might step in a puddle and get squelchy shoes. You might come last. So what? If you stop trying for an instant in judo, you get slammed into the mat, smothered, strangled and get your arm bent backwards to breaking point. I knew when I was onto a good thing.

Before long, I began to enjoy running. I liked the feeling of getting fit again after a period of slack. I progressed quickly from two miles to three, four and five miles. Soon I was on the school team. While I was never going to be a star, I learned to love running and many years later, it became a vital part of my martial arts training.

When I left school I spent a year abroad, doing nothing much, as you do at that age. But by the time I got back to Blighty, I was beginning to feel restless.

Life was less stressful without sports and martial arts, but it was less rewarding too. There was a complacency in me that I didn't like. It felt alien after all those years of effort. I missed the incredible sense of worth I used to get from facing the challenges of judo.

I like to think it was my spirit, crying out to be forged strong and true by some classical martial arts training, but it was probably just vanity. I liked being different. A bit special. A martial artist.

Whatever the reason, by the time I began life as a student, the martial arts were beginning to lure me back with their awful, irresistible song.

London Calling

When it was time to apply for university places, my teacher told me not to bother with London.

'Too many distractions for the likes of you, Powell,' he warned.

For some reason, I listened to this banal advice and applied for places in other cities instead. But London and I were destined to be together and in the end, the Tao provided.

I failed to get the grades for a place at a fine university in a quaint English town, and ended up in a scruffy South London poly. The distractions were only just beginning.

On the first night at the dorm, I propped up the bar, trying hard to look relaxed. Thankfully, the other students were all in the same boat. They turned out to be a friendly bunch. We soon got talking. The topic never wavered. Where are you from? What are you studying? What A-levels did you get?

It was all fairly straightforward until I noticed a bit of a commotion at the bar. The chap next to me had asked for blackcurrant in his bitter. John the Barman, a beer-purist complete with 'Real Ale' T-shirt, was clearly appalled but indulged him nonetheless.

I recognised the guilty party as my new next-door neighbour, Tony. We got talking. He was half Nigerian, half Irish, and all Liverpool. Tony was several inches shorter than me, but built like a pocket battleship. I asked him which he did, rugby or bodybuilding? He told me he was a brown belt in karate.

We became friends. We'd often go out in London with a gang of students from the dorm. After a couple of pints of beer and blackcurrant, Tony would show off to the girls by doing one-handed chin-ups on a bus shelter, or jumping high into the air and kicking the roof. He was always a big hit with ladies, who must have been bored with the rest of us weedy intellectuals. At parties they were practically lining up to feel his bulging muscles. When it was time to get the last bus home, he never came with us. He was always 'busy'.

One day, while Tony and I were waiting by the lift to go down to lunch, we began play fighting. I'd never done any kicking or punching, but it came quite easily. 'You're not bad,' Tony told me, as we bounced around the foyer. The lift came and went.

We continued for ten minutes until Tony's control slipped slightly and he kicked me in the face. Right across the nose. My eyes misted over. Tony wanted to carry on. I told him I'd had enough.

'No,' he laughed, 'this is your chance to get me back. C'mon, let's do a bit more.'

'Fuck off,' I said, sullenly. There was a stony silence in the lift as we went down to lunch.

But a few days later, I went with Tony to a local karate club. He was easily the best student, but he was more interested in partying, and rarely trained. I began to go on my own, but Tony was always next door and helped me with the basic moves.

I stood in the correct stances and learned how to kick, punch and block. Soon I was doing my first kata. It was a simple sequence of movements and I learned it easily.

The classes were very tame compared to judo. I was surprised, because karate was considered a far more deadly martial art. Could it really be that simple? I doubted it, but I was curious enough to continue for a little longer, just to make sure.

We would do touch-fighting for a few minutes and then some kata practise. I was amazed to see some of the senior grades panting and kneeling on the floor. How could they be so tired from such an easy exercise? This was hardly the warrior spirit I was expecting.

The instructor told us he was going to teach us to love pain. It spooked me for a while. I expected some terrible new exercise, but it never came. In fact, it all seemed so *painless*. The only real danger was lack of control. There was always a chance someone might hit you too hard in the face by accident. I don't recall any major incidents.

By the end of the year one, I'd reached orange belt. On reflection, I decided my dad was probably right. Karate was a bit easy. I doubted how effective it would be in a proper fight. Maybe I was missing something?

After first year exams, I set about finding accommodation for next year. The dorm was kicking us out to make room for the next batch of students. My girlfriend and I decided to rent a large property with five other students. We searched around North London and settled on a big dilapidated place in Seven Sisters, South Tottenham.

It was here that I stumbled across a very different karate club. The instructor didn't promise to teach me to love pain. In fact he hardly said two words to me in the years I trained with him. But he did teach me how to handle pain and succeeded in changing my opinion about karate, almost overnight.

First Contact

Soon after we moved to Tottenham, there was a full-scale riot. We heard police helicopters overhead and watched in amazement as the TV showed an angry mob just around the corner from our house. It was the Broadwater Farm riot.

A couple of weeks later the drug squad raided our house. A package of hard drugs had been detected at Dover. Our address was on the front. Perhaps on the back it said 'If undelivered, please return to the Golden Triangle'.

They allowed the package to be delivered to see what would happen, staking out the house and watching as the postman made his delivery.

Luckily my flatmate Paul refused the package because it was not addressed to anyone by name, so we avoided a full-scale search. In the end, several officers simply came in and questioned us for an hour, drank a few cups of tea, and left. We were safe, but the whole episode scared the hell out of another flatmate, Bill, who hadn't even had time to flush his seeds down the loo.

We soon settled into the area despite all the drama. One night when things were a little quieter, I decided to check out the local karate club. I'd seen the ad in the local paper. It was just a short bus ride from my house.

I took the No. 259 down the High Road and got out just before White Hart Lane. I could smell fried onions. The road was filled with crowds and scruffy men were frying hamburgers at little pavement stands. There was a football match. Mounted police and dog handlers were everywhere. The atmosphere was tense, especially since the recent riots.

I pushed my way through the crowds and into the local sports hall, where I presented myself to the instructor, Joe Claronino. He was smaller than me but powerfully built, with a mop of wavy dark hair and strange grey-green eyes. They seemed to be laughing, but otherwise, he was quite serious.

I told him I wanted to join and I was already an orange belt. He said I'd have to start again because they did a different style of karate. Perhaps he didn't believe me? I offered to bring my certificate as proof. He wasn't interested. He insisted, quite calmly, that I would have to start again at white belt.

To add insult to injury, he told me I'd have to train in the beginners' class for three months, until I was ready to join the main class. I was disappointed, but part of me was also curious. What was so special about this man's karate? I decided it couldn't hurt to find out. How wrong can you be?

I got changed and joined a line-up of maybe 15 other beginners. Some were in tracksuits, while others, like me, had done something before. We wore the traditional white '*gi*' of the Japanese martial arts and a white belt that indicated we were the lowest of the low.

The class wasn't taken by Joe Claronino, but by his most senior student, Gary Malcolm. We were told to address him as *Sempai*, which means 'senior'. Sempai Malcolm was tall, with a square jaw and rippling muscles. He looked extremely fit.

He took us through some basic warm-up and stretching exercises. I noticed a big difference straight away. There was a definite sense of purpose here. No resting and chatting between exercises. He was counting in Japanese which seemed a lot more authentic than counting in English. I noticed how repetitive the count was and guessed he was going from one to ten, over and over. And over and over…

'Squats! *Ichi, ni, san, shi*…' We did maybe fifty squats, until our legs were burning.

'Press-up! *Ichi, ni, san, shi*…' He told us to make a fist and do the press ups on our knuckles. The front two knuckles of each hand. We were on a wooden floor and our knuckles skinned almost immediately. 'Don't worry,' Sempai Malcolm assured us, 'you'll soon get used to it.' Our arms trembled as we struggled to do ten agonising press-ups.

'Sit-ups! *Ichi, ni, san, shi*…' We sat, facing a partner and interlocked ankles. Then the count began. It seemed never-ending. We did maybe a hundred sit-ups. By the end, we were holding onto our trousers and pulling ourselves up with our arms, grunting in pain.

Then we moved onto basic techniques. Punches. Kicks. Blocks. Stances. Mercifully, they were similar to what I'd learned before. But instead of doing a set of ten and having a little rest, we continued up to 50 before moving straight onto the next exercise.

After an hour we were exhausted. Sempai Malcolm took us through some stretches to warm down. Then we knelt in a line and he spoke calmly to us.

'Don't worry that we didn't do very much today,' he told us sincerely. 'We'll build up to more over the next few weeks. You'll soon be ready to join in the main class.'

I was amazed. He wasn't joking. How could people do more than that? Surely it was impossible? I waited behind to watch the main class and see for myself.

Soon a mass of young men and women began arriving and warming up in the *dojo* (training hall). They all looked fit and strong. Some were very flexible and sat in the splits or propped one leg high against the wall.

When the class began, I peered into the dojo through a small window. It was steaming up rapidly. Sensei took the class through a thorough warm-up, making sure every muscle was properly stretched. Even the toes and heels got a massage, before he moved onto more serious exercises.

Soon the pace began to pick up. Sensei had the class punching relentlessly and shouting loud '*kiais*' in unison. The noise was immense, and echoed around the building. The walls were shaking. It went on and on, until they had done well over a hundred punches. Eventually they moved onto hundreds of blocks before doing endless kicks. There was no rest and no respite.

I could see Sempai Malcolm at the front of the class, leading by example. They were doing straight-leg kicks, high in the air. Hundreds of them. His leg was going like a bloody metronome. I'd seen enough to understand what he'd meant earlier. I had a long way to go.

I was excited and a little awed by the standards at this club. I wondered if I had what it takes to join the main class.

I turned up again on Thursday and the next Monday. I don't think I missed a single class for the next three months. I was totally hooked. By the end of the beginners' course only four were left from the 15 that had started. We were all a similar standard, young, fit, serious and more than a little worried about joining the main class.

Sempai Malcolm was as good as his word. He had us pumping out press-ups, sit-ups and squats like there was no tomorrow. We knew all the basic punches, blocks and kicks. After class, we'd kneel in a line and he'd answer our questions patiently. I began to learn about karate.

I had no idea there were different styles. We were training in a full-contact style called *Kyokushinkai*. In practice, that meant we were allowed to punch hard to the body and kick the legs, body and head. Head kicks were expected to be controlled. We soon got used to a certain degree of contact as a matter of course and my forearms were black and blue from blocking punches.

My thighs and shins were constantly sore from the low kicks. These were new to me. My previous style only taught kicks above the waist. Low kicks were a revelation. They were relatively easy to do; you don't need to be super flexible and they were devastatingly effective. A low kick impacts onto the thigh with the hard bone of the shin. It's amazingly painful. It feels like getting the classic 'dead leg' that you might remember from school.

Sempai Malcolm took some time to explain the etiquette of the main class. He reminded us to bow on entering the dojo and again on leaving, even if the place was empty. We had to bow to the instructor before addressing him and bow to our partners before training with them. I discovered this was simply a mark of respect and acknowledgement in Japanese culture, not an act of subservience.

I could understand bowing to a person, but bowing to an empty room didn't make sense. However, I'd learned to respect Sempai Malcolm's views and I was in awe of Sensei Claronino, so if they wanted me to bow to an empty room, so be it. It was only many years later that another instructor helped me understand the value of this gesture.

Sempai Malcolm told us to address Joe Claronino as 'Sensei', which translates loosely as 'teacher' in Japanese. He advised us not to bother Sensei with trivia. Sensei was not interested in idle chitchat.

I soon realised that our relationship with Sensei was not the same as the usual student/teacher relationship or even athlete/coach. A *Sensei* is different, something else, a remote figure; part teacher, part captain, part mentor, part father…

We were polite and respectful to Sensei at all times, especially inside the dojo. We were encouraged to speak only if we had a sensible question, or needed to inform him of an injury. Otherwise, the only word we really needed was '*Osu!*' (pronounced as a forceful exhalation: Ooouussss!) I discovered that '*Osu*' was a fantastic, multi-purpose word. It could be used to mean, well, *anything* really…

'Do you understand?'

'*Osu!*'

'Does anyone *not* understand?'

'*Osu!*'

'Shout when you hit the pad.'

'*OSU!*'

'Thank you all for training so hard.'

'*Osu!*'

I learned about the grading system. There were ten levels of coloured belt, and ten levels of black belt known as *dan*. Sempai Malcolm was a second dan, which made him a class senior, a form of senior prefect. A karate practitioner is normally considered a fully qualified instructor at third dan, and is then addressed as 'Sensei'.

Sensei Claronino was a fifth dan, which is the first master grade. Some time later, he was awarded the official title of *Shihan* (master).

I learned that my Sensei coached the British Knockdown team. What was this *knockdown* I kept hearing about? I discovered it referred to the unique tournament rules of Kyokushinkai. As the name suggests, two people fight until one is knocked down. There are no points for any kicks or punches unless someone ends up on the floor, so little is left to the opinion of the referee or the imagination of the audience. Like most things in my new karate club, it seemed harsh but fair.

This was all light years away for me. My only worry was my first grading and what I needed to do to get my belt. That time came all too soon. On the day of the grading I was quite nervous, but I knew Sempai Malcolm had prepared us well. We were all strong and fit. I was armed with my little black book of the Kyokushinkai syllabus, which set it all down nice and clear. I made sure I knew all the techniques I needed.

As we entered the dojo for the grading there was something different about the place. Sensei had made things a bit more official by borrowing a table and chair from the office. There were people from other clubs here too. I eyed them nervously, wondering how good they were.

Sensei called the grading to order and we bowed. Then he began calling out techniques and making notes on his piece of paper. It was disconcerting. I tried to ignore it and concentrate on what I was doing. After half an hour, Sensei told us to put on our shin pads. It was time to spar.

This was always the hardest part for me; the struggle against other people. By nature, I disliked confrontation. However,

I was willing to stand up for myself, if need be. And I really wanted this belt.

I turned to face one of my usual training partners. We fought hard and fast because neither wanted to look weak, or as if we weren't trying. I kept my hands high to avoid getting kicked in the head. Anything else, I was prepared to take.

We changed partners and I turned to face one of the guys from another club. He was tough but a little slow. We exchanged a few good shots, but he didn't give me any real trouble. I was used to training with some better people.

Then Sensei moved onto kata. He called us out one by one. We needed to perform one simple kata, but with the rest of the class watching and Sensei making notes on his sheet of paper, it was all a bit hair-raising.

One chap began his kata... one step, two steps... then he froze. He looked to the ceiling for inspiration, then shook his head in despair. His mind had gone completely blank. Sensei shouted at him to begin again. This time he stumbled through the kata with a couple of stops. It was a right old mess. I looked on in horror. Could I remember the kata now, in front of all these people? I told myself I could. It would be crazy to go through all that fighting and then fail the grading on memory loss.

My legs felt hollow and shaky as I took my place in the centre of the dojo. Sensei called out '*Hajime!*' for me to start, and I blasted through the kata without a hitch. I wasn't going to go through all the rough stuff and then fail on the easy bit.

We moved onto the fitness test. I pumped out the required number of press-ups, sit-ups and squats and then Sensei called an end to the grading. We lined up expectantly but Sensei made no announcement. We had to wait until the next class to find out if we'd passed.

On Monday, I learned that I had. I was allowed to wear my orange belt again. This time when I wrapped it around my waist, it felt different. Very worthwhile.

I'd discovered a karate style that was a struggle, just like judo, just like the occasional real fights I had in the street and the playground. But unlike my judo club, which had been quite an amateur affair, this was the real deal. I was training under one of the UK's top instructors, in the style that confidently called itself *the strongest karate*. I would be joining the main class next week. I wondered if I could I handle it?

The next Monday, I crept into the dojo and stood at the back of the class. There were three or four rows of higher grades in front. I hoped I wouldn't embarrass myself.

The class began gently with a good warm-up, but soon enough we were punching hard and fast. The count seemed to go on forever. But the energy in the room was infectious and I managed to keep up. Next, Sensei got out some large pads and we kicked and punched them as hard as we could. My knuckles didn't stand a chance. They were already scabby from the push-ups and the skin just burst off.

I hit the pads until I felt sick and gasped for breath. Then we practised kata, over and over, with no break. Finally we began the ritual that took place at the end of every lesson. Three sets of 50 push-ups on the bloody mess that used to be my knuckles. Then 300 sit-ups, facing a partner. The only consolation was that we were allowed to sit on our shin pads, to spare our arses on the wooden floor.

Sensei would often add a set of squats, in his own unique style. The class would all count ten each, starting with Sempai Malcolm and going down the line. The count would begin loud and clear in Japanese. Sensei was happy for us to count in English if we needed to, but needless to say there was always someone who couldn't count to ten in either language! This would throw the whole class into confusion and Sensei would scowl. If the delay went on longer than a few seconds, he'd make us start again from the beginning. By this time, our legs would be in agony and even the black belts would turn round and glare at the fool. We soon learned to count to ten.

We trained two evenings in the week and again on Sunday mornings, when there was a five-mile run to 'warm up' before the class. I ran it in a respectable time, thanks to the geography teacher who made me do cross-country, but I found walking straight into a class and doing 200 kicks a different matter. My legs seized up. When we did press-ups, I was too tired to do more than five. I still had a long way to go in my fitness.

I trained religiously three times a week and began to notice improvements. I always tried hard, but when my energy levels began to flag, as they invariably did, I would simply tuck in at the back of the class and let myself be pulled along by the tremendous spirit and enthusiasm of everyone around me.

The person responsible for this great atmosphere was Sensei himself. He was a strange and enigmatic figure. He rarely spoke to me, or anyone else, although he did share the occasional joke with Sempai Malcolm or one of the other black belts. But the man knew how to set a class alight and generate immense energy. This helped us push ourselves beyond what we considered our limits.

Occasionally on a Sunday, when Sensei and Sempai Malcolm weren't around, Carl would take the class. He was a brown belt who'd begun competing in Kyokushinkai's infamous 'knockdown'. Carl would bring his skipping rope along and we'd all jump in time with him. You must work on your fitness, he warned us. You must push yourself as hard as you can, every time you train.

When I got home my flatmates were just getting out of bed. I'd regale them with the rigours of our training. They'd look at my bruised arms and bloody knuckles like I was crazy. Doing that much exercise as a student was seriously uncool. I told them about Sensei and how we had to do whatever he said without question. Then they would take the piss: *'Would you walk out in front of a bus if Sensei told you to?'*

At the back of my mind, I knew they did have a point. I found myself in a confusing situation. As a student, I was supposed to be a freethinker, not a mindless automaton. At the poly I was surrounded by people with strong socialist ideals: anti war, anti Nazi, anti Thatcher.

The lecturers I admired were liberal intellectuals who showed us the dangers of obeying strict doctrines like fascism and communism. Meanwhile, at my karate club, I was being told to obey commands without question. I was drilling up and down in strict militaristic style. I was being told to ignore pain and tiredness and to 'never give up'. I was learning to beat people up, maybe even kill them. I began to question my conscience and tried to train without letting myself get brainwashed into becoming part of the machine.

It didn't work. If I thought about what I was doing, the training quickly became too painful to continue. I had to buy into it wholeheartedly, or not at all.

I was far too hooked on karate to give up. But there was another thing that helped to make my mind up. I looked at the characters of the people teaching me, Sensei Claronino, Sempai Malcolm and other seniors like Carl, and realised that I had rarely met such admirable people. If they were a product of this kind of training, I decided it couldn't be wrong. So I took Carl's advice on trust and it didn't fail me.

I gave myself up to my training. As the count went on, and on, and the pain got worse and worse, I would resist the temptation of hoping it would end. Instead, I would look forward to the next ten. I stopped huffing and puffing and began to affect the air of nonchalance that I'd seen in the higher grades. Each lesson became a private battle with Sensei. No matter what exercises he set, I refused to show him I was tired.

This attitude worked well for me and later, as we began training for knockdown tournaments, we were encouraged to develop this 'fuck off' attitude. After a hard sparring session, or a long blast on the pads, we were forced to stand up straight with our hands clasped over our heads. No one was allowed to bend over and put their hands on their knees, let alone lean on a wall or sit down.

We learned that during a fight, you give off signals that your opponent can read. So if you're tired, it's important not to show it. Don't huff and puff and look sorry for yourself. There is no need. It doesn't help you in any way, but it will encourage your opponent to make one last effort and finish you off. Of course, it works the other way too. If you see *him* looking exhausted, you can feel encouraged. You can gain strength from it and finish him off.

I was discovering how to fight the psychological battles that take place in a physical confrontation.

I realised your spirit is like a pilot light, burning inside you. No matter what happens to your external self, how battered and beaten you are, your pilot light can still burn brightly. Your opponent can never reach in and blow it out. Only you can do that. It's always a choice.

Having said that, my pilot light did flicker once or twice, during those early days in the main class. Some of us beginners were taking a regular hammering from the higher grades. I never suffered too badly myself, but there were some who got a hell of a kicking. At first I felt sorry for them. But when I observed more closely, I noticed something interesting. It wasn't the weak ones who were getting hurt. It was the cocky ones and the clumsy ones.

These guys were getting knocked about because they were going in too hard against the higher grades. Perhaps they thought the brown belts and black belts felt no pain? Or perhaps they didn't like someone getting the better of them, even if that person was far more skilled. Either way, they were hitting too hard, and getting punished for it.

I never suffered too badly because, even as a beginner, I had good control. I never swung out wildly without any thought for my opponent. I never lost my temper when somebody caught me with a good technique. I just accepted it and tried to block it the next time. I was happy to learn from the higher grades. Every high grade except one: Floyd.

Floyd was the person we feared most. He was a black belt, as thin as a pin, very flexible and very fast. He always took exception to getting hit by a lower grade and would retaliate by knocking them down with a head kick. I would regularly hear a thud and look round to see a figure slumped at Floyd's feet. Sensei would warn him to be careful, but Floyd couldn't help it. He just got carried away.

I did my best to avoid him, but you can only hide for so long. One evening we were called out to fight in front of the class. I was determined not to get kicked in the head. I held my guard high and told myself 'watch the head… watch the head… watch the head…' It was no use. Barely a few seconds had gone by before a blinding pain exploded across my nose and everything went black. Next thing I knew, I was sitting on my arse.

Floyd helped me up good-naturedly. I wanted to disappear to the changing rooms and run cold water over my face, or at least sit to the side like a wounded warrior. But Sensei made us continue. There can be few things in life more miserable than fighting on after being kicked in the face. I felt weak and sick and thankfully Floyd went easy on me for the rest of the match.

I realised Sensei had made me continue deliberately. He always tried to avoid finishing a match on an injury. He would wait until the injured person had recovered enough to fight a little longer, to help develop the right spirit. In Kyokushinkai, spirit was everything.

Throughout my second year at college, my spirit got stronger. I was able to train longer and harder than ever before, and withstand more pressure than I could have imagined even just 12 months earlier. But my training was about to take a new direction. My next year at college was going to be spent abroad.

One day, shortly before my departure, I told Sensei I would be leaving for a year. I promised to return to the club as soon as I got back to London. He wished me well, but I'm not sure he believed me. If he didn't, it was understandable. He must have heard it all a hundred times before.

Spanish Lessons

My course at the polytechnic included a year abroad. It would be a chance to immerse myself in the culture and language of two countries, Spain and Germany. I'd been looking forward to these foreign placements for a long time. I'd get six months in Valencia and then six months in Stuttgart.

I'd never been to Spain before. I wondered what it would be like. My mother is from former Yugoslavia, so as a child, I spent the summer at my grandmother's house in Montenegro. My only knowledge of Spain came from what I'd read in books. George Orwell painted a depressing picture of the horrors of the Spanish Civil War. I studied Spain under Franco and its isolation from Europe. It seemed the country had been a backwater for many years. As I boarded the plane for Valencia, I had a very confused idea of what to expect.

When I landed, my preconceptions vanished. Instead of finding a dirt road, a donkey and a little pueblo, I found I had arrived in one of the most beautiful and vibrant cities I'd ever seen. It was midnight, in the middle of October, and the temperature was a balmy 18 degrees.

The taxi driver told me there was a heatwave, but that was all I could understand. He took me into the centre of town, passing high palm trees, whitewashed villas and old castle walls. Neon signs winked their advertising messages at me. The place reminded me of Italy, which I'd visited once as a child. It had that unmistakeable Mediterranean smell in the air. I fell in love with it instantly.

I booked myself into a dingy hostel in the town centre and began looking for a flat. I bought the local paper and searched for a *piso estudiante* (student flat). Then, with several numbers circled, I headed down to a pay phone. I lifted the receiver and called the first number. A woman answered brusquely: '*Digame!*' I stumbled out my request for information. A torrent of Spanish came down the phone. I mumbled '*Gracias, adios*' and replaced the receiver.

Clearly I'd spent too much time in the dojo and not enough time in the language lab. It took me four more weeks to find a flat. I ended up sharing with three English guys from my course.

Once we were safely installed in a small tidy place near the university, I set about the next important matter. Finding a karate club. I was amazed to find Spain had Paginas Amarillas (Yellow Pages) and searched for sports clubs. To my surprise, I found a karate club listed nearby, and better still, it was Kyokushinkai. I was curious to see how it compared.

I walked over that evening to take a look. It was a brand spanking new sports club complete with a well-equipped weights gym. The dojo was large and beautifully decorated, with mirrors down one entire side, and Japanese posters and scrolls hanging on the wall. There was even a receptionist to meet and greet clients. She introduced me to the two Senseis who ran the club, Arturo and Pepe. They were both third dans.

They invited me into their office and we talked for a while. It turned out they knew a good deal about Kyokushinkai in Britain, and had even heard of my instructor, Joe Claronino. They told me they were training to become international referees, but were struggling because their English was poor. Of course, most of the commands for fighting were given in Japanese, but it was important to know certain phrases such as warnings in English. They gave me an example.

'No crapping,' said Arturo.

'I'm sorry?'

'No crapping!' repeated Pepe.

'No crapping!' said Arturo, more forcefully.

Did they really need to warn people against that? Perhaps they could place a discreet sign at the edge of the mat, like they do for dogs in the park?

Pepe pulled at his sleeve. 'Crapping…'

'Oh, you mean *grabbing… No grabbing!*'

In knockdown fights, it's illegal to grab your opponent's suit and hold them while you strike. I explained the difference and we all had a laugh.

Then Arturo had an idea. He offered me free training at the club in exchange for English lessons. I readily agreed, as money was very tight. We sorted out my membership form there and then.

The karate classes were smaller than in Tottenham, about half the size, but there were still a couple of black belts. I was impressed with the general fitness and spirit. If I'd expected the Spanish to be a bit laid back in their training, I was very much mistaken. They were a tough and friendly bunch and I felt at home straight away.

The warm-up and basics were familiar and soon we put shin pads on for sparring. Arturo called '*Hajime!*' (begin) and left us to it. In the heat the sweat soon began pouring off us. The finely polished floor quickly became an ice rink. We sparred for about half an hour. Thanks to all the hard training I'd done in London I held my own and was one of the last to tire.

I was thankful for my fitness. I was beginning to realise how important it really was. It could make the difference between getting away relatively unscathed or getting seriously hurt. If you're unfit, you can easily end up at the mercy of your opponent. If you're sparring you might get a battering. If you're in a tough grading or a tournament you risk a serious beating and you're more likely to get knocked out. In the street, fights are often over quickly but it's good to know that if it drags on, you won't be the first to tire.

Two days later, I returned for our first English class. Arturo brought an old textbook and we worked through some examples. Then we went through some phrases for a referee. After 30 minutes, my new students became restless and Pepe offered to show me around the weights gym instead. I had not done weights before, but I knew it was a good supplement to Kyokushinkai. I readily agreed.

He showed me a good routine and since I had plenty of free time, I began weight training in earnest three times a week. I was already fit and I made rapid gains in my strength. My chest filled out with a bit of muscle, which pleased me immensely. I was a bit scrawny in those days.

I wondered whether weight training would tighten me up and slow me down, but since I was still doing plenty of karate and stretching, I found it had the opposite effect. My punches were faster and harder than ever. Pepe also showed me how to use the heavy bag, and I used it to warm up before doing weights.

We had two more English classes before their interest waned. Whenever I turned up the guys would be late, or busy, or 'out'. No problem. I headed straight for the gym and had a good workout instead.

My flatmate Vince was mad on bodybuilding and he joined a specialised gym. He knew a lot more about pumping iron than I did, and gave me advice on developing my lats, traps and delts (back, neck and shoulders). He'd show us his bodybuilding magazines, and we'd laugh at the obscene amount of muscle on the guys, and girls. Vince would read his mags to psyche himself up for training, and then leave in a flourish, shouting 'Ah'm gunna fuckin' *wreck* my pecs', slamming the door behind him. He'd come back several hours later, barely able to move.

Mark was a middle distance runner and ran for an athletics club in London. He was taking it easy while in Spain, but he did train occasionally. One day I went with him. We jogged over to the university track and he introduced me to one of the most painful but useful exercises for martial arts. Sprints.

Although Mark competed in races over a mile or more, he would often train by doing sets of 400-metre sprints. I'd heard Sebastian Coe did this sort of thing as part of his training and I was interested in how it worked.

Mark explained the theory. If you prepare for a one-mile race by running one mile, your body is not truly prepared for the pace of the actual race. That's because we always run faster in a race than in training. Our bodies are operating at a pace that's faster than they have experienced in training.

By running at a faster pace over a shorter distance, the body becomes accustomed to this higher work rate. It doesn't come as such a shock to it. Of course, there is the need to sustain this work rate for a longer period during the actual race, but this can be easier than trying to run the entire race faster than your normally run.

That was the theory and it made sense to me. I realised this had happened many time during my cross-country days. It was not the distance that killed me. It was the pace. I was well aware how quickly I became breathless during a hard sparring match. Anything to improve my fitness was most welcome.

The 400 metres is often described as the 'man-killer'. I discovered why. Mark and I jogged a couple of laps to warm up and did some stretching and striding exercises. Then we took our places on the starting line. Mark checked his watch, counting down, 'Three, two, one, *go*!' We set off at a blistering pace. I stayed right behind him around the first bend. Then we reached the back straight and he went forwards while I went backwards. There was nothing I could do. By the third bend my body seized up completely. My breath came out in strange, choking gasps. My legs turned to jelly and I resisted the urge to puke. Meanwhile, Mark's lithe figure was streaking away down the final straight. I saw him casually check his watch as he crossed the line. I shuffled the last 100 metres and collapsed.

We walked a lap to recover and set off again. We did three more fast laps. Mark seemed to get better each time but the first one had killed me and I spent a lot of the time jogging. I was amazed how sprinting could take you from readiness to exhaustion in a matter of seconds.

The human body can only operate at 'maximum' for around thirty seconds before it begins to slow down. I felt these sprints recreated the tiredness of sparring far more accurately than a five-mile run, so I went to the track a couple more times and practised on my own. I felt I'd discovered a new secret weapon.

My third flatmate, Phil, was not into sports. He was quiet and unassuming. He told me he was a singer.

'What sort of music?' I asked.

'Heavy rock, heavy metal,' he replied casually.

I was surprised, as Phil was always immaculately attired in freshly pressed slacks and a polo shirt. If the evening became fresh, he would occasionally don a fine Pringle sweater. He just didn't seem the type. I'd brought my guitar and we sat down together. Blimey, the man could sing. He sounded like David Coverdale and Jon Bon Jovi rolled into one. It turned out that Vince played bass and Mark played guitar and flute. We began writing songs and jamming together.

One evening, soon after we moved in, we decided to check out the nightlife in Valencia. We asked several trendy looking people where to go for the best bars. They all told us the same square, called Canovas. We went to Canovas and found it empty. After several beers, we decided the Valencia nightlife sucked and got up to leave. Just then a handful of young people began to arrive on scooters. The bars filled up. Cars were soon parking two and three abreast around the small square. The place was heaving.

We got talking to some pretty girls. They introduced us to their boyfriends, who scowled at us but said nothing. The girls invited us to go to a nightclub. Let's go, we said. *Vamos!* They giggled. It was far too early. It didn't really get going until 3 a.m. An hour or two later, we went along to the District 10 nightclub, and ended up coming home at dawn.

As we walked back to our little apartment on the Calle de Sagunto, the bakery downstairs has just opened up. The smell of freshly baked bread enticed us in. We bought four large loaves and devoured them, still warm, with butter and marmalade. Valencia didn't suck after all. We'd just forgotten that like most civilised countries, Spain was not constricted by silly licensing laws. They kept very different hours, especially over the weekend.

Towards the end of my stay in Valencia, I took a grading at the karate club. It was tough but straightforward. I passed. I was a yellow belt.

I wasn't sure whether Sensei would recognise my grade when I returned. I'd have to wait and see. If he did, I'd be half way to black belt, at least on paper. In reality, I knew there was still a long way to go. The next five belts would be a lot, lot tougher.

Beer and Schnapps

After six months in Valencia, I flew back to London. I had a couple of days before heading to my next placement in Germany. There was no time to visit my beloved club in Tottenham. I was too busy catching up with my girlfriend and packing my winter woollies.

The weather in Spain had been beautiful in the winter. Even on a cold day, there was always bright sunshine and blue skies.

Stuttgart, in February, was a different story. It was everything Valencia wasn't. The city seemed grey and uninviting. Dirty snow lay piled up at the roadside. I was miles from the centre of town and none of my friends were there. They all went to France instead.

But soon I began to see the bright side of Germany. Instead of having to find a flat for myself – no mean feat in a foreign country – there was a room waiting for me in a student dorm. After a little Teutonic paperwork, I was given the key to a room in apartment block 42A.

The building was ugly, but the room was warm and comfortable. Better still, I bumped into other students from London who were finishing their stay in Stuttgart. They introduced me to their friends and showed me around. There was a bright, fast underground train nearby that ran into the town centre every ten minutes. It was so reliable, you could set your watch by it.

This wasn't so bad after all. A few days later the rest of the students from London arrived, including Joanna Mills, who was to become one of my closest friends. We got to know two Germans who seemed to like the 'Tommies', as they called us. They were Peter and Thomas, who had a great sense of humour, and stood out from the rest of the German student population like a couple of sore thumbs.

Yes, the German students were a curious bunch and we Brits never tired of laughing at them. Some would walk around in white shirts and black waistcoats, complete with torn jeans, bandana and sandals. They seemed stuck in a hippy time warp and weren't embarrassed to talk about yoghurt being good for the digestion. Some didn't even have a 'look' and wore check shirts, pullovers and cords. Several even had beards!

My friend Peter had recently been elected the 'leader' of block 42A and took his responsibility very seriously. His official title was 'Haus-meister' (House-master) but we insisted on calling him 'Haus-fuhrer'. His sense of humour usually failed him at that point and he would give us a puzzled, longsuffering look.

One day, he led me to the fridge and showed me a list of names stuck on the door. My name was there too.

'Zo,' he began to explain in English (he liked to practise), 'if you want to take one beer, you must put one mark next to your name, on the list, like zo…' and he did a tick. Then he opened the door to reveal a fridge full of fine German lager. It was like a scene from one of those beer commercials where a lad's dream comes true.

The really amazing thing was, the system worked. The Germans would tick their names as they took a beer, and pay up dutifully at the end of each month. I tried to imagine the same in England. Yeah, right.

Whenever there was a shortfall, Peter would knock on my door and ask, very patiently, whether I'd 'forgotten' to tick the box? (Well, it's easy to lose count after the first couple, isn't it?)

Once I'd settled into my digs, I checked the Gelbe Seiten (good old Yellow Pages) for karate clubs. There were plenty in the town centre, but the only Kyokushinkai club was on the outskirts, a good hour away. I called the number, but there was no reply. I decided to go there in person. I was determined to avoid other styles if possible. I had a dim view of their standards.

So, one freezing February evening, I wrapped myself up in a long overcoat and took the S-Bahn train to the other side of town. The journey took 45 minutes and I walked for another 20 minutes before arriving at the address. There was no sign of any club. The snow was falling steadily and the place was utterly deserted. I trudged back forlornly, arriving at the student dorms late, frozen and dejected.

At the university, I saw a poster for karate. The style said Shotokan. Everyone was welcome. I went along, rather sceptically. I found a first dan black belt and four beginners. The black belt was delighted to have me along. He explained he'd only started the club recently. He felt he had already learned enough about karate and now wanted to help others by becoming a teacher.

I was suspicious. I knew that although a black belt is a great achievement, it is not until third dan that someone is regarded as a fully-fledged instructor. Sadly, my suspicions were confirmed. He took one of the lamest classes I have ever experienced. I could have done better myself. Afterwards, he urged me to come back regularly. I murmured something non-committal and ran.

Now I was at a loss. I checked the Yellow Pages again and saw an ad for karate at a gym called Top Fit. It was conveniently placed for me on the train-line, but when I rang, they told me it was Shotokan. I decided to give it one last chance. After all, I had to do something.

I went along that evening to meet the instructor, who was a third dan. He was tall with long grey hair swept back and a magnificent handlebar moustache. He was a big hard bastard, no question. I felt a little more confident already. He explained how the classes worked. He taught the basics and kata classes while his assistant instructor, Rudi, taught the free-sparring sessions. There were two sparring classes per week.

I asked if I could attend the sparring only. I explained that I was only there for six months and didn't want to start a new syllabus from scratch. He said that would be fine, so I arranged to come to the sparring lesson on Monday.

I wasn't sure what to expect, so I got there early. I wanted to get properly warmed up and ready to defend myself. When you visit a new dojo for the first time, there is always the chance of a tear up. The better fighters will sometimes test you to see what you've got. They want to see where you fit in the pecking order. Since I came from a different style, there was a chance they would be especially hard on me.

I introduced myself to Rudi, who was tall and powerful, and mercifully devoid of moustache or beard. Though he was only a first dan, his black belt was worn almost white with age, which indicated he'd been around the block a few times. Later he told me he had never been interested in becoming an instructor and concentrated solely on competitions.

The class was big, maybe 25 students of various grades, from beginners to black belts. Rudi took us through some good warm-ups and we did a few sets of press-ups, squats and sit-ups. The level of fitness was good, but not quite as high as I was used to.

Then Rudi showed us sparring techniques, one after another. We worked in pairs, practising the reverse punch, head kicks, sweeps and back-fist strikes. After a while, he called for *jiu kumite* (free sparring) and we were off.

I started with someone about my own grade, and we fought well together. I was not used to having punches aimed at my face. They were getting through far too easily. Also, in this style of sparring, low kicks were not allowed. I missed them and their simple effectiveness. But I forced myself to adapt to their methods. My opponent darted in and out and caught me with some good techniques, but I managed to tag him a couple of times too.

We changed partners and I teamed up with a brown belt. This guy was not particularly fast, or good, and compensated by laying his punches in very heavily. I tried to keep it light and friendly, as Rudi had instructed, but this guy's face was twisted into a scowl and there was a blank look in his eyes.

He came in hard a couple more times, and I began to get annoyed. I waited until he was passed close to the wall and closed the space between us. Now he could not back off and I slammed a couple of hard shots into his stomach and ribs. I knew I could hit a lot harder than he could. Now he did too. The scowl came off his face and was replaced by a more neutral expression. We sparred quite happily after that.

I became a regular at Rudi's classes and enjoyed them immensely. It was not exactly the karate I wanted to do in the long run, but I was very happy to train this way for the time being. I could see Rudi was a master at what he did, and I picked up lots of hints and tips about this style of fighting. I learned to be faster on my feet and to cover ground quickly, lunging in and out of an attack. I learned to strike with more accuracy. I was looking forward to going back to Tottenham and trying out some of my new skills on the Kyokushin boys.

I used the weights gym too and my strength continued to improve. One afternoon, I decided to give my legs a big workout. I did five sets of squats, working up to bigger and bigger weights. I totally wrecked my quads, as Vince would have said. I hoped Rudi wouldn't be doing squats that night in class.

Well, maybe Rudi saw me training and decided to teach me a lesson, or maybe the Tao decided to play a cruel joke on me, but that night we did literally hundreds of squats. Rudi had a whole array of nasty new leg exercises for us (some of which I still use to this day). My legs burned. My muscles screamed. I was in agony, but did my best to stay with the count. After the class, I tottered up the stairs and hobbled home as best I could.

It wasn't until the next day that the full horror struck. Overnight, my muscles had stiffened up and I couldn't get out of bed. The slightest movement was agony. Walking upstairs was unbearable. Walking downstairs was unspeakable. I plodded around the campus like a mummy for the next five days and ended up missing nearly a whole week of precious training.

I never made the same mistake again. From then on, I made sure to keep my training more general before a class. I would only target specific areas afterwards.

I discovered a running track near the dorm. It was empty most of the time. The German students were not the fittest bunch. Their idea of health was a bowl of muesli. I did 400 metre sprints, just as Mark had shown me in Spain. I began keeping a record of my times and tried to beat them by a couple of seconds each go. Soon I was able to sprint the whole way round and push through the barrier that always hits around the three-hundred-metre mark. This is the place where your body can't operate at 100 per cent any longer.

Overall, I was pleased with my gains in strength and fitness, until the day my friend Thomas invited Joanna and me to spend the weekend at his parent's house. They lived an hour north of Stuttgart in a tiny village in the countryside near the beautiful river Tauber.

His parents welcomed us warmly and cooked a special meal. We took a fiery shot of schnapps before we started. Then they poured us several glasses of local white wine with the heavy main course. His mother had cooked lots of delicious cakes for dessert and insisted we try a piece of each. It would have been rude to refuse. By the end, my belly was full to bursting.

Thomas's father was an elderly gentleman farmer. Thomas told us he needed to help his dad with some chores the next morning. Did we want to come along? We were non-committal, until he told us we could ride on a tractor. That was an offer we could not refuse.

In the end, with Thomas and his dad already aboard, there was no room on the tractor so Joanna and I sat on the trailer instead. It was filled with straw. The tractor took off with a sudden jolt and we overbalanced, so Jo rolled in the hay with me (though she denies it these day, of course).

After a short drive, we stopped at a cowshed. Thomas and his father each took a pitchfork and began tossing bales of hay from the trailer to the shed.

'Hey Goran! You are strong...' said Thomas.

I made appropriately modest noises.

'Here, have a try,' he offered, smirking.

Well, I did fancy myself as something of an athlete, so I spiked a bale and tossed it into the cowshed. It was heavier than I'd imagined. I tossed two more and my back began to ache. Meanwhile Thomas's elderly father was flicking the bales over his head like a machine. I huffed and puffed until Thomas took pity on me and finished the job.

I realised how specific fitness is. You become good at what you do. Your body develops the strength and flexibility to cope with the exercises you set it. After a while, it develops muscle memory. Then it can perform a task automatically, without conscious thought. This natural, instinctive movement is what fighters are looking for. There's no time to think. In a fight, your body needs to react instantly.

A fighter develops muscle memory by spending many hours working on drills for footwork, kicking and punching and balance. It's also important to hit something like the heavy bag or hand-held pads to get the feeling of actually making contact.

During the long winter days in Germany, I felt isolated from my London club and took to reading books and magazines about karate. I read about the founders of the two styles I knew. Shotokan was founded by Gichin Funakoshi. I read his book *My Way* (actually *Mein Weg* because I read it in German).

I enjoyed his humble, scholarly style. He was a small man, a teacher and calligrapher. Though a highly trained karate master, he wrote proudly of how he avoided using his skill against ignorant people who pushed him around. This image of the warrior poet appealed to me: a man who knows devastating techniques but keeps them permanently hidden from view. It seemed very noble. Very Zen.

The founder of Kyokushinkai was, in many ways, his opposite. Masutatsu Oyama was a large and immensely powerful man. He got his black belt in Shotokan under Funakoshi and also trained in another major karate style, Goju Ryu, under the famous master Yamaguchi. Eventually he grew disillusioned and felt neither style was exactly what he wanted. After a period of intense training and meditation in the mountains, he came back to civilisation and founded his own style: Kyokushinkai.

His ability was truly awesome and he did many famous public demonstrations of his skill, breaking wood and bricks, even fighting bulls and chopping off their horns with his bare hands. He toured America and took on all comers. He was never beaten and rapidly became a legend in Japan.

He admired Thai boxers for their toughness and fighting spirit and added Thai boxing techniques such as thigh kicks to his syllabus. He developed his own full-contact tournament rules, *Knockdown*, which quickly became popular with fighters and audiences for its exciting battles.

His fame spread around the world and people came from all over to train in his Tokyo headquarters. One such person was Steve Arneil, who was the head of the British Karate Kyokushinkai. He travelled from his home in South Africa to train with Oyama and was the first person to pass Oyama's ultimate test, the Hundred Man Kumite.

He fought 100 men, one after another, in a marathon fighting session that lasted several hours. It was a feat that very few have ever equalled. Even to this day, there are only a handful of names on that honours list. Many more have taken shorter tests like the Thirty, Forty, or Fifty Man Kumite, pushing their own personal boundaries to new limits.

Oyama was an inspirational figure to me and I used him to motivate myself while training alone. I had a five-mile course through the woods and timed each run. I tried to beat my record each time. The final mile was a long, straight avenue through the trees where I would feel most tired. I tried to push hard for the finish line, but with no one to race against, it was tempting to slacken off. Then I would imagine Oyama, looking down at me from above the treetops. If I pushed hard he would nod approvingly. If I slackened off, he would look away in disgust. Maybe even spit on the floor. I tried my best not to disappoint him.

This was the first time I used mental images in my training. It worked well. Many years later, I began to study mental attitude in more depth, and researched how top boxers build up a strong mind. I found they used systematic techniques of visualisation and verbalisation to condition their minds for success. Later, when I used these methods myself, I found they delivered some powerful results. But for the time being, I was still more interested in simply getting fit.

One evening, towards the end of my stay in Stuttgart, a new black belt turned up to Rudi's class. He had a cocky air about him which I disliked from the start. However, he seemed to be tight with Rudi, so I assumed he was one of his tournament buddies. By this time I knew everyone in the class, and although I was by no means the best, I was certainly no pushover.

After a good warm-up, Rudi told us to spar. We all fought a few rounds, but when it came to this guy, it was obvious he had something to prove. He launched hard attacks from the very first second. I was good enough at this type of sparring to play these guys at their own game, and attacked equally hard and fast in return. He seemed surprised, as I was wearing a yellow belt, which signified a lower grade in his style than in mine.

We exchanged a flurry of kicks and punches. It was so fast, I could barely see what was happening. Things were a blur. Then

I heard a loud crack and everything went dark. He'd punched me hard in the eye. I turned away, stunned, and Rudi came over to stop the fight. The black belt was apologetic and suitably embarrassed. They checked my face. My eye was already puffy and closing over, but my big worry was my contact lens.

I held my eyelid open and asked if they could see the lens on my eye. They couldn't. I assumed it had fallen out and we searched around the mat for a while in vain. Eventually, I said not to worry, I would get a replacement. Rudi sent me upstairs to clean myself up. I checked my eye in the mirror. I was going to have a hell of a shiner in the morning.

The eye was red and watery. I felt something bothering me under my eyelid. I realised it was my contact lens. It had been knocked out of place by the punch. I tried blinking to get it down, but it was no use. I rubbed my eye and blinked and blinked. Eventually, after many minutes, it came down far enough for me to pinch it out.

Those were the days before disposable lenses. A new lens cost around £50 so I didn't want to lose it. My eye was far too sore to reinsert it, so I popped it in my mouth instead. A lens needs to be kept moist or it will dry out and crack. I made my way up to the bar and explained what had happened. Did they have a little jar I could use to fill with water and transport the lens home? After much searching, all they could give me was a clear plastic bag.

I went home on the train carrying my precious cargo on my lap. The lens was invisible in the bag of water. The people opposite gave me curious glances and who can blame them? I must have looked like some nutter who'd won an invisible goldfish at the fair.

The Knockdown

When I got back to London for my final year at college, I wasted no time in returning to my club in Tottenham. If Sensei was pleased to see me back, he hid it well. But he did allow me to keep the yellow belt I'd got in Spain. I like to think he could tell I'd been training hard while I was away.

Over the next 12 months, I took two more gradings. By the time I finished my degree and joined the ranks of the unemployed, I was a green belt.

After a month or two, I got my first job. I was a translator. The pay was terrible and it was miles away in Croydon. I had to work shifts, so I couldn't always get to training. Thankfully, I'd learned to train outside the dojo, so even if I missed a class, I made sure I did something.

My friends and I had rented another big, dilapidated house, but this time we'd gone up in the world and moved to Highgate. I checked a map of the area for parks and places to train. I went on a couple of exploratory runs, checking out the best routes to avoid the traffic and fumes, looking for green areas like parks, football pitches or sports grounds where I could work out.

In the end, I settled on a quiet road not far from the house. It was on a steep hill that led to the back of Highgate station. I started at the bottom and sprinted to the top. It took a little over a minute, just long enough to really, really hurt. Like the track sessions, I did four sprints and jogged down each time. Once when I was feeling extra keen, I jogged over to Muswell Hill and sprinted up a couple of times. It was much longer, a real killer, but it was always busy with traffic. I didn't like the idea of gasping in the fumes and returned to my quiet hill near the tube.

I also searched for a gym. In the end I settled on a place a few stops away on the Northern line in Camden. The thing that clinched it for me was the heavy punchbag that hung there permanently. I was beginning to think bag work was the ideal exercise for martial artists, combining strength, stamina and technique, plus conditioning the hands for impact. The only downside is, as Bruce Lee said about boards: they don't hit back. You need to guard against complacency in your footwork and defence.

There were plenty of other martial artists training at the gym. Some wore star-spangled outfits or colourful Thai boxer's shorts. One chap, in a simple T-shirt and tracksuit trousers, impressed me with his strength and fitness. Unlike some of the others, who tapped and posed on the bag, he tore into it with his bare fists, sending the heavy bag jumping and swinging wildly with his force.

We eyed each other suspiciously for several weeks, until one day he asked me what style I did.

'Kyokushinkai,' I said, nonchalantly.

'You're joking?' he said. 'That's what I do. Or used to do…'

We introduced ourselves. It turned out Roy was a brown belt who had lost his way. He didn't want to go back to his club until he felt strong enough. He seemed plenty strong enough to me, but he lacked confidence.

We began training together and soon became firm friends. We would warm up and do some *kihon* (basics) together. Then we'd spar for several rounds, hit the bag and push weights. Roy was always stronger than me, which forced me to try harder and do more than before. He would 'spot' me, standing near as I attempted a heavy weight, and just use his fingertips to assist me on the last couple of reps.

When my girlfriend and I moved to a small flat of our own in Walthamstow, it turned out Roy lived a few streets away. We began to meet on the playing fields nearby. People walking their dogs would see Roy and me kicking the shit out of each other, sprinting between the trees and lying in the wet grass doing sit-ups. They must have thought we were insane, but being British, they never batted an eyelid.

Roy was like a machine. He loved the physicality of a good workout. His strength was always better than mine, but when it came to cardio work like running, I had a slight edge. We would take it in turns to choose an exercise and do the count.

Ichi, ni, san, shi… We began to compete to see who could devise the most painful workout.

One day, Roy decided to resurrect an old training exercise from the past. He referred to it simply as 'The Flats'. I assumed he meant sprinting on the Wanstead Flats, which was a vast expanse of playing fields nearby. Err, no… He pointed to a block of flats near the Hackney Marshes. As we jogged over, he explained the rules.

There were 21 floors in the skyscraper. He'd been there before. He would start on the first floor. I would start on the ground floor. We would run up the stairwell as fast as we could. My task was simple: I had to catch him before he reached the top.

'What about the residents?' I asked, incredulously. 'won't they be a bit pissed off, with two nutters racing up their stairwell?'

'Nah. Don't worry about that,' he reassured me, 'nobody leaves their flat in that place.'

I shuddered. When we got there, the place really seemed deserted. Some of the doorways were boarded up. The stairs were dark and stank of piss. Nobody had even bothered with graffiti.

Roy took pole position on the first floor and shouted '*Go!*'. I exploded up the stairs three at a time and flew up the first four flights. Then gravity began to take its toll. My pace slowed. I took the stairs two at a time, legs burning, gasping, choking. Then one at a time. When I finally reached the top, I was close to a coronary. Did I catch Roy? I really can't remember. I was too knackered to care.

We swapped places and went again. Roy wrecked himself trying to catch me. I don't think he succeeded. We made our way down and out into the fresh air. Nobody came out to complain. We didn't see a single soul.

To this day, I can't think of a harder exercise, but we never went back. It was just such a miserable experience that neither of us suggested it again. Roy was content with the unspoken fact that he'd won the 'most painful exercise' competition.

Back at the club, Sensei had his own painful exercise in store for me. At the end of a typically gruelling class, he went to his kit bag and returned with a notebook and pen. He announced there was a knockdown tournament coming up in Folkstone in a few months' time. He wanted names. He reminded us green belts were eligible to enter. The silence was deafening.

He reassured us that it was a regional competition, not national, so it would be a good place to start. Some of my clubmates had already taken part in a 'novice' knockdown tournament, which was, in theory, even easier. They had done quite well, but I'd been abroad at the time. There were no more novice tournaments on the horizon, so I resigned myself to being thrown in at the deep end.

Sensei wrote our names in his book. He assured us entry was voluntary, but he seemed to be operating an 'opt-out' policy rather than 'opt-in'. Basically your name was down unless you told him otherwise. I couldn't think of any good reason not to enter, apart from being terrified. And even so, there was another part of me that was eager and excited. I knew I was seriously fit. All the extra training with Roy meant my sparring was sharp. It would be interesting to put it to the test and see what happened.

We formed a squad of about eight people, mainly green belts like myself. Sempai Malcolm was our coach. During class, Sensei would work us extra hard. At the end, he'd put us in a line and make us continue sparring. Eight people would come out to fight us. The others would rest. Then another eight would be called out. They'd be fresh, while we were getting more tired.

At weekends, the squad would meet for extra training on Hampstead Heath. Sempai Malcolm had us sprinting up the hill and doing jumping burpies at the top, over and over, until we were ready to puke.

In the weeks leading up to the tournament, I thought of little else. Roy was keen to help me prepare and we stepped up my training. He would yell at me to try harder. Since I was the one competing, it was down to me to do more than him every time. It wasn't as difficult as I'd expected. The thought of the tournament had got me so pumped up that my adrenaline was racing. I found it easy to push myself to new limits.

I had no car, so Roy offered to drive me and my girlfriend to the tournament in Folkestone. It had been a hell of a long time since I'd done a tournament. The last time I'd been a kid, driving up with my dad. I remembered the feelings of dread as we drove up the motorway, and anticipated something similar for my first knockdown. But even though this was potentially more scary than a judo tournament, I found I wasn't as nervous as before.

It was not simply about being an adult, either. This time I knew I had prepared correctly. While I knew I was not as skilful as some, I knew one thing for certain: there would be no one fitter than me. This gave me a deep-seated confidence and self-belief that made the journey quite bearable. I also knew that as a novice fighter, there was little pressure on me.

But when we reached the sports arena, my heart sank. I looked at the other competitors and noticed a lot of familiar faces. Where had I seen them before? At the National Championships at Crystal Palace, that's where. This tournament was not restricted to London and the South East. There were fighters from all over. Shit, even the Welsh were there. No one liked fighting the Welsh; they were always very tough. Fighters had flown in from abroad: France, Germany, Holland. So much for Sensei's 'regional' competition.

I weighed in at exactly 70 kilos (11 stone) and made it into the lightweight division (Those were the days.) I tried to work out who I'd be fighting. They all looked pretty scary. Some were pacing up and down, shadow boxing and kicking, while others were sitting nonchalantly in the splits, chatting to their friends or instructors.

I warmed up and stretched, waiting for my name to be called out. I hated the waiting. My palms were sweating and butterflies were running riot in my stomach. My mouth was constantly dry but as soon as I sipped water, I needed a piss. Soon I was longing to be called out to fight. Anything was better than waiting. Then I was told I had a 'by' into the second round, so I had to wait even longer.

I sat with my girlfriend and Roy. There was a fight going on in front of us. One big guy was really kicking the shit out of a much smaller, weaker guy. It seemed a total mis-match. It was painful to watch. Soon the weaker fighter was completely battered and unable to defend himself. His opponent smashed through his guard and kneed him in the chest. There was a crunching sound and the little chap crumpled onto the mat. He was clearly not getting up and the first aiders from St John's Ambulance were called. They took one look at him and brought a stretcher. There was no sign of life apart from the occasional twitch.

My girlfriend was duly shocked. Was this what I was about to do? She had never seen karate before and must have assumed my stories had been somewhat embellished. This was *barbaric*, as bad as boxing. Her illusions of karate as a noble martial art were shattered forever.

Yet she quickly developed a macabre fascination for it and called my attention to a fight on another mat.

'Look at that black belt,' she said excitedly, 'he's amazing! He keeps jumping up and twirling around and kicking them in the head.'

Sure enough as I looked over, he spun around and caught his opponent with a perfect hook kick. His heel connected with the other guy's temple. St John's Ambulance hurried over with their little red stretcher.

'I'm glad you don't have to fight him,' she said, loud enough for the Tao to hear. And of course, the Tao responded. Within minutes, the announcer called me out to fight him.

Sempai Malcolm gave me the low-down on my opponent.

'He's a third dan and he fights in the British team,' he told me. *Yes, thanks for that little nugget, Sempai.*

'His main technique is the spinning back kick…'

Yes, I've noticed that already.

'Keep your hands up and watch out for that kick. You'll be fine.'

I nodded. What else was I supposed to do?

I looked over and saw the guy bouncing confidently, with a small smile on his face. He was shorter than me, but he looked very strong. I guessed we weighed about the same. I held his gaze for a moment. I didn't care who he was, or what belt he wore. I was determined he wouldn't find me such easy prey.

As I walked onto the mat, my legs got that familiar shaky, heavy, watery sensation. I ignored it and continued to look just beyond my opponent. I was very aware of his attitude. He was still bouncing confidently. He wasn't trying to eyeball me, but

I felt he was trying to disconcert me with his casualness. Well, I could be casual too. I caught his eye again and gave him a hint of a nod and a smile.

The referee called us to our markers. He made us bow. Then he motioned for us to begin and shouted '*Hajime!*' but there was a roaring in my ears so loud that I registered no words or sounds. It was the rush of pure adrenaline filling my body. The next thing I knew, I was fighting.

I lunged forward and hit my opponent with everything I had. To my surprise, most of my punches and kicks got through. He wasn't trying hard to block or hit back. He simply absorbed them for a while, waiting for me to finish. Then, in a blur, he whipped around. At the last instant, I realised that kick was coming. I jerked away. It was too late. He caught me on the ear with his heel. I stumbled forward and into him, catching hold of him to keep myself up.

Fortunately my last-second reaction meant I escaped the full force of the kick. It was not enough to knock me over. My ear stung like hell, but otherwise, I was fine. Enraged, I charged forward to get him back and ran straight onto a perfectly timed spinning back kick. It hit me straight in my belly and stopped me dead in my tracks. The air went out of me, and I felt sick. But again, it was not enough to knock me down.

From then on, I engaged him more cautiously, and we traded simple body shots and low kicks for a while. Every so often, he would spin around and try to take my head off, but I was attuned to the technique now, and moved into him, making him miss. I was not going to fall for the same trick twice. Eventually he got frustrated and even jumped up in front of me, trying to land a simple roundhouse kick to my head. Again I smothered him and caught him with some good combinations.

I began to grow in confidence. I was doing just fine. Soon, I heard the sound of the hooter which signified we'd been fighting for one and a half minutes. There were 30 seconds until the end of the round, and no score. Neither of us had been knocked down.

He'd come closer to achieving a knockout, but I felt I had landed more punches and kicks. We engaged in another furious exchange and I landed five punches to his four. I was pleased with myself. I was giving a highly ranked fighter a good run for his money. Perhaps I might even win? Just at that moment, as my mind was entertaining this happy thought (instead of concentrating on the fight) his fifth punch came home. It whipped around my guard and smashed into my liver with sickening force.

If I'd seen it coming, I'd have been OK. I could have tensed that side of my body and rode the punch. I could have breathed out, to avoid being winded. But it had caught me completely off guard. The breath left my body. I gasped and hunched over.

The referee stopped the fight. I was bent double, fighting for breath. He strode over to me and asked if I was able to continue. I nodded and rose to my feet. What else could I do? He called us back to our starting lines. Before we began again, he awarded a half point to my opponent. We fought on for a few more seconds and then the bell went. The guy had a half point, which was enough to win him the match. And so ended my first knockdown fight.

Sempai Malcolm was delighted with my performance.

'You did fantastic,' he assured me.

My teammates came over to congratulate me. I was dazed, not from the kicks or punches, but from the sheers nervous energy of it all. I felt like I'd taken my first skydive, or gone down the Colorado rapids. It wash an incredible rush. During the fight, I'd developed a form of tunnel vision. I had been oblivious to any sights or sounds from my surroundings. This had helped me survive, until that momentary lapse in concentration when I came unstuck.

I was reasonably happy with my performance against a seasoned opponent. But I was also annoyed with myself. I'd made a silly mistake and lost because of it. Part of me was glad I didn't have to wait for any more fights. The waiting was the worst part. Another part was annoyed that I'd had such a difficult draw. I had seen a lot of fighters who I thought I could beat. It would have been good to win at least one fight.

We stayed to watch the rest of the tournament. My opponent duly won the gold medal. I think he knocked out every one of his opponents with his fantastic spinning kick, which made me feel a little better about things.

When we went home in the car, my body began to ache. My chest and ribs were bruised. It hurt if I breathed too deeply. My hands were sore. I realised it was from the impact of my own punches. My ear had swollen up. I wondered if I'd be left with a cauliflower ear, like a grizzly old wrestler.

I played the fight over in my head. I was surprised that my fitness and determination had compensated almost entirely for my lack of experience. It had taken a top fighter almost two minutes to find a way through my defences and seriously hurt me. He had not been immune to my punches and kicks. If I hadn't made a silly mistake and lost my concentration, I might have gone on longer. I might have even won.

I realised fitness is the bedrock of a fighter's ability. It breeds confidence, determination and fighting spirit, which can make a huge difference. These simple things can compensate for some lack of technical ability. But in the end, he had outsmarted me, switching from one technique to another and catching me unexpectedly. This was a level of skill and know-how that takes a lot longer to acquire.

My mental attitude had been good. On the whole, I was pleased with myself. I had not been psyched out by what I'd seen. I had fought to the best of my ability, better than I had ever fought before. I could not really expect more of myself.

I realised that the waiting had been the hardest part. The worst part of the whole tournament. How I hated it. The anxiety. The nerves. Or let's call it by its real name: *the fear*. I needed to find a way to cope with the fear. Was there any way? It would take me many more years of karate to answer that one.

When the fighting started, it had come as a blessed relief from the waiting. It had been quite liberating, almost fun. For the first time, I'd been given free reign to hit someone with all my might. As long as I stayed within the rules there was no need to worry about hurting the man. Quite the opposite. I had licence to hit him as hard as I could, as often as I could, as long as I could. The only downside was he had the same licence.

I wasn't to know it then, but this day was a major turning point in my karate. I was much more confident afterwards, because I proved a lot of important things to myself. I didn't crumble under pressure. I could raise my game. I could go toe-to-toe with a top fighter and take the hard shots (as long as I saw them coming). In those two short minutes of fighting, I lost a lifetime of doubt and gained a new level of self-belief that has stayed with me ever since.

And this is how you make big leaps in martial arts. It's not the same as normal progress, which is straightforward: you train, you rest, you improve. Mental and spiritual leaps come from particular experiences and moments in your life. They are usually fairly instant, like Zen enlightenment. Suddenly, something dawns on you. The penny drops. A veil is lifted and you see things in a new light. A better light. Hopefully, one of those things is yourself.

The Pit of Despair

We're back at the campsite. The sun is beating down hard, just like last year. We've moved from the Field of Truth to a more sheltered spot at the bottom of the hill. It's seen its fair share of blood, sweat and tears too. The annual grading takes place here. The instructors like to call it the Pit of Despair. They haven't lost their mean sense of humour.

Mark and Charlie are about to attempt the Thirty Man Kumite. Two long lines have formed for them. One line of men, one of women. Charlie is the first female in the association to attempt the test. (Apologies to the PC among you, but I can't bring myself to call it the Thirty Woman Kumite. It just doesn't have the right ring to it.)

Charlie is also Sensei Gavin's wife, which is something of a mixed blessing. He has helped her train with fitness workouts and sparring, but it's been a strain on both of them. As one of her examiners, he will need to be scrupulously fair during the test. Poor Charlie must have wondered if she'd get things extra tough, just so Sensei could not be accused of favouritism.

One week before summer camp, I'd been talking with Gavin and Charlie after a class. Charlie's mind was in turmoil. She was worrying endlessly about who would be in her line-up. She worried about fighting guys and being kicked in the head. And she worried about fighting Kaz, a large, powerful Maori girl who was a bouncer in one of London's seedier locations and a real force to be reckoned with. Gavin occasionally sent her to the back of the dojo to sort out some of the cockier new guys, believing that getting a pasting from a girl was a good way to learn humility.

Kaz wasn't due to be in the line-up, but Charlie worried about it nonetheless. She wanted Gavin to confirm who would be fighting her, but he wouldn't tell her. It would not have been right or fair. No one knows their line-up until the day. It's all part of the test. You fight whoever they put in front of you.

Still, Gavin clearly felt bad about the whole situation (and I doubt he ate any hot dinners that week). Charlie was sick with worry. She was literally puking up in the toilet. When I spoke to Gavin later in the week, we both wondered whether she would bail out. Physically, she was in great shape, with years of experience and months of special training under her belt. Mentally, she seemed to be coming unstuck.

The day before summer camp, I got a phone call from Gavin. He told me Charlie had approached him quite formally and requested that Kaz be included in her line-up. This pleased Gavin immensely. At last, she'd got her head together. She was ready to cope with the awful thing he was going to put her through.

During the first two days of summer camp, Charlie stayed calm and focused. Something had clearly clicked inside her. She'd decided she was going to do it. She was ready.

And now is her moment of truth. Her line is quite short. There are not enough highly ranked girls to make a line of 30, so she'll have to fight some twice, and probably some guys too.

Mark's line is much longer. There are plenty of strong fighters assembled and we've been joined by three jujitsu black belts, two first dans and their instructor, a third dan. This is going to be interesting. Near the end of the line, Steve is waiting. I take my place at the very end. I'll be Mark's last fight.

Mark is one of the strongest, most talented fighters I have ever come across. For someone weighing in the region of fourteen stone, he's very fast. In fact, he rivals Carl as perhaps the strongest fighter in the association. They've certainly had a few epic battles in the past.

Today, he's looking calm and composed. He's chatting with Charlie and they give each other a final hug before taking their places opposite their line-ups. I wonder what it must feel like, to face 30 people? Mark's line stretches the entire length of the glade.

The instructors check with the timekeeper. Is she ready? She is. We all bow and the first fighters step out. The fighting starts.

Mark looks very sharp. His first few opponents are made to suffer. He uses his vicious front kick to knock them backwards and keep them at bay. Mark is equally happy close up, where he throws hard body shots and low kicks. When one fighter goes in hard against him, Mark knees him in the face. The fighting is stopped and the man is given time to recover. I look over to see how Charlie is doing. She's fighting skilfully, keeping up a steady work rate of punches and kicks, moving nicely to avoid getting caught.

Mark's fights are more of a tear-up. But after five fights, he's beginning to lose his freshness. Now his opponents are succeeding in putting him under pressure. When he attacks hard with low kicks, they grab hold and wrestle with him. Mark is a good grappler and manages to throw them to the ground, but the pushing and shoving is beginning to tire him out.

Each new fighter is fresh and more experienced than the last. Now they begin to test Mark. The pace is often furious. In the heat of the struggle a couple of stray punches catch him in the face. The fighters are not cutting him any slack.

Meanwhile Charlie is working systematically. She seems to have found an even pace and sticks to it. She avoids clinching and grappling and doesn't move too far around the field, to conserve her energy. It looks like she's trained herself to simply punch and kick non-stop for 30 minutes. This rhythmic striking is making it difficult for the girls to get in close and hurt her. I make a mental note for future reference.

By the time of his first break, after ten fights, Mark is looking tired and dishevelled. He's annoyed about being punched in the face. He and Charlie exchange a few words of encouragement and sip their drinks. Then the fighting resumes.

Mark starts with some new freshness, but after two more fights, he's beginning to flag. He's being caught with punches, kicks and throws that he would have evaded easily in normal circumstances. The Thirty Man Kumite is stripping him of his normal defences. Time after time he's caught by hard punches and low kicks. He's taken to the ground. But while Mark is very tired, he's still dangerous. If someone comes in too hard, he retaliates with his own hard attacks.

When the jujitsu fighters come out, their tactics are clear. They don't want to stand and trade with an excellent striker. Their strength is grappling. They grab hold as soon as they can and take him to the ground. Normally the instructors stop the fighting once it goes to the ground, but they let things go on a little longer to put Mark under extra pressure.

Though the jujitsu guys are expert grapplers, they are still unable to dominate him. And once they're standing up, Mark begins to deal with them in his own sweet way. He holds them at arms length and slams low kicks into their legs. It works. But by the time he has fought all three of them, he's totally spent.

At this stage he comes up against several of the biggest and toughest guys in the association. They hit him again and again with crunching low kicks and hooks into the ribs. Mark uses all his skill and every last ounce of energy to keep himself in the fights.

I glance across to Charlie, to see how she is doing. I know I should be watching her fights more closely, but I can't avoid watching Mark instead. This is the division where I fight too, and I'll be fighting Mark myself soon. I want to see what he's got.

Charlie's fights are very different. She has kept up an astonishing work-rate of kicking and punching. The girls have had trouble putting her under pressure. Her continuous combinations have made her hard to pin down, and though she looks quite tired now, she still seems remarkably composed.

The Pit of Despair

After 20 fights Charlie and Mark get their second and final break. They sip their drinks and encourage each other, but the break is over all too soon. Once the fighting resumes, I know I'm only a matter of minutes away from my fight. I begin to hop from one foot to another and throw a few combinations to warm up. I know he might still be dangerous, especially in his last fight.

Indeed, he has started with a little extra freshness. But soon he's taking a pounding again. Now he's among the strongest black belts, and they are hitting him with full force, smashing into his bruised legs and hooking big punches into his stomach and ribs, and down onto his chest.

Mark fights with his elbows close together to protect his ribs. Though he wants to fight back, his body is too tired to work properly. By now it's clear he's exhausted. It's spirit alone that's keeping him going.

I look over to see how Charlie is doing. She's still going like a little machine, albeit slower than before. Her hands and feet look heavier now. The instructors have sent a few guys over to liven things up a little. They put her under new pressure and she's hurting, but she hasn't lost her composure. Every so often she brushes a stray hair off her forehead.

Mark is not such a pretty sight. His top is hanging open, along with his mouth, and he is gasping for air. His arms hang idly by his sides. Since his line-up was only 28 people, Gavin has made him fight two of the club's toughest fighters again. Now it's Steve's turn. This is bad news for Mark.

Steve is tall and exceptionally fit and strong. He's also very determined, and hammers away mercilessly at Mark's legs. He smashes the left leg, two, three, four times on the same spot. Mark buckles. He grabs hold to avoid falling and Steve smashes an immense punch into his stomach. There is a moment of stillness. Mark's air leaves him. His face is contorted in pain and slowly, he begins to double over. Steve stands back for a moment, waiting to see what will happen. Is Mark going to fall?

The crowd scream at him to continue, and through the fog, perhaps he hears them. He ignores the pain and forces himself to stand up straight. He knows he's near the end of his test and wants to finish without being knocked down. The crowd yell their support, willing him on for one more effort. Steve tears into him again, smashing his leg remorselessly. Jesus, Steve, does he owe you money?

Time is called, and Mark has reached his last fight. Although I know he's an exceptional fighter, I can see he's dead on his feet. I jog out to him. It will be like taking candy from a baby. The instructor shouts 'Hajime!' (begin) and I test Mark with a few careful shots. Then he explodes with a two-punch combination and a huge low kick into my left leg. I feel it buckle and struggle to keep my balance. I can't believe he has so much power in his exhausted state. Well, if that's how you want to play it Mark, fuck you too!

I slip to the side and bang a couple of hooks into his ribs, moving in and out of range too quickly for him to catch me again. Now he covers up, fighting with his arms close together. His elbows are almost touching, so I can't get any punches to his body. That's fine. I'll take a different target.

I hammer five or six vicious punches into his upper arms, digging my knuckles into the muscle with a nasty little hooking action. I can feel the bone. He still insists on covering his body, so I attack the legs, to keep him guessing where the attacks will come.

I switch back to his arms. I hammer another five or six shots into his biceps and triceps. This battery of strikes is keeping his arms pinned to his sides and soon they're too dead to work. I circle him, hooking a nasty little punch into the kidney. He grunts in pain, but he won't go down.

His big attack used up his last drop of energy and now he's fighting on empty. Too tired to kick and virtually unable to punch, he fights on pure willpower, staying with me and refusing to cave in under the pressure.

Finally, the timekeeper yells 'time' and the instructor calls 'Yame'. We don't hear it. Sensei Gavin rushes between us, waving his arms to stop. It's over. I jog back to my starting point to end on a formal bow. I'm breathing hard after just one minute. What must Mark feel like after 30 minutes?

He hobbles and gasps, drawing in long, deep, painful breaths, his face twisted in pain, his clothing hanging untidily on him. Sensei Gavin walks proudly alongside him as they make their way slowly to our starting position. We bow. He has done it.

I shake his hand and congratulate him with a hug. I'm awestruck by his achievement. Charlie had succeeded in her test too. She's had some very tough fights towards the end, and is not looking quite so fresh now. I think I even spotted a hair out of place.

The instructors call things to order, and the two fighters take a formal bow to their line-ups. They're mobbed by a crowd of well-wishers, hugging and kissing them, shaking their hands and congratulating them.

No one is happier, or more relieved, than Gavin himself. His wife has completed the test safely, with nothing worse than some nasty bumps and bruises. He's immensely proud of her, and awards her one of his oldest and most precious black belts as a gift. It's worn and straggly, faded to a mottled grey (a sign of years of training) but the name embroidered on it in gold silk is still clearly visible: G Mulholland. This is a nice touch, because it's also her name: Genevieve Mulholland. (Charlie is just a nickname.)

That evening by the campfire, Mark showed me his upper arms. They were both covered in nasty bruises.

'Why did you keep hitting me in the arms?' He asked.

'You had your body covered up. I answered. 'I thought you didn't want any more body shots. I was doing you a favour' I offered, 'anyway, it was the obvious target...'

'My body was fine,' he complained. 'I could have taken some more. I couldn't hit you back because you kept hitting my arms!'

There's no pleasing some people, is there?

Neither of us knew it at the time, but Mark would be able to get his own back on me in due course. And on Steve. He'd done his Thirty Man Kumite.

We still had ours to come.

The Knockout

I'd finished my studies, and it was time to consider my career. What the hell was I going to do? I had no idea. When we joined the European Union, I'd assumed British companies would be crying out for linguists. By the time I graduated in languages, I'd be gold dust on the job market. Some chance. The Brits continued their time-honoured tradition of speaking to foreigners in pidgin English, and shouting if they weren't understood.

I went back to my poorly paid job as a translator. It was not the illustrious career I'd had in mind. So I decided to try my hand at something else. I checked the press for sales and marketing jobs. There were a couple that said 'second language useful'.

I got an interview at a printing factory that made wrapping paper. Europe was their main market. They told me my languages would be useful, but first I'd have to learn the trade. It seemed reasonable to me and I said so with all the enthusiasm I could muster. The prospect of a five-figure salary was whirring before my eyes like a cash register. To my surprise, they offered me the job. The salary was £10,250; three grand more than I was getting at the time. I jumped at the chance.

So began my training in that great British institution: the factory. Each morning I arrived in a cold, drafty building by the Bow flyover, donned a pair of grubby overalls and steel toecap boots and began my rounds of the printing presses. I took a sample of paper from each machine for testing. What did this have to do with European sales and marketing? I had no idea, but my boss assured me it was a vital part of my training.

His office was upstairs. It was fairly spartan by most standards, but sheer bloody luxury compared to my little workshop. I quizzed him about my prospects. When would I start going to meetings, flying to Europe (business class, of course) and driving a BMW? He said I needed to do six months on the factory floor before they would begin grooming me for stardom.

I never met the owner of the firm. The only sign of him was a huge green Volvo parked outside. One morning, I got a message that he wanted something collected from Stratford – the nearest area of civilisation. They told me to use his car. I had a licence, but I hadn't driven for years, and never in London. What would happen if I scratched his car? I pictured the scene:

'Knock, Knock…'

'COME!'

'You wanted to see me?'

'Who are you?'

'Err, Goran Powell…'

(blank expression)

'I work here… the new Sales and Marketing Executive… trainee?'

'Oh, it's you! You're the bugger who scratched my car! Well, it's coming out of your wages! Every penny! It's going to cost over £10,000 to fix that door. You'll have to work for nothing for a whole year.'

'I don't suppose this is a good time to ask when we're going on our first European assignment together?'

Needless to say, I bottled it, and one of my colleagues drove the bloody Volvo to Stratford. After a few months of this miserable existence, I decided it wasn't the job for me. I began searching for a new position with a few more perks like a desk and chair, perhaps even a radiator.

A friend of mine was doing well in a financial services company in the West End. She told me there was a job going in the marketing department, and put my name forward. I got myself suited and booted and, to my surprise, I got the job. It even paid a little bit more. The creature comforts were all there. I had a nice big desk, a leather chair and central heating. The office had a door, instead of plastic sheeting.

But the pressures were there too. This was the late eighties and *greed was good*. Things kept changing at breakneck speed. My first boss left soon after I joined. Her replacement came from Saatchi & Saatchi complete with Filofax, Mont Blanc pen and Porsche Carrera (soft top, naturally).

He wasn't too sure about me. Every so often he would pull me aside for a little chat. He'd tell me at Saatchi's, trainees like me would sweat blood to get their careers off the ground. I needed to put more effort into my work. I needed to care. I listened to what he was saying, but I didn't really hear.

I was doing plenty of sweating, but only in the dojo. There was a tournament coming up in Oldham and that was all I could think about. I'd leave work at five-thirty sharp to get to karate, or meet Roy at the gym. Or I'd jog to an empty stretch of road near home and work on my sprints long into the night.

This level of intensity made training far from enjoyable. It was painful. But I wanted to prepare myself as fully as I could. I knew every ounce of pain I felt in training would be an ounce less during the fighting. Fitness was everything to me. It was my only protection, my insurance policy against being badly beaten.

I was often tired at work and sore from the training. I had little energy or enthusiasm. My main interest was not work. It was food. I needed plenty of calories to keep up this level of training. By mid-morning I'd open my sandwich box and begin munching. At lunchtime, I'd pop out for a big plate of pasta, or rice and chicken. By four o'clock I'd be ready for a final snack to tide me over for training.

The prospect of a tournament was a curious thing. It made me nervous, but it helped me train harder than ever before. Each time I thought about it, I'd get a small adrenaline rush, and I'd find myself training harder. I was more aggressive, more determined. I began actively seeking out the hardest fighters in the club for sparring. I knew it would stand me in good stead later.

One evening, I found myself face to face with Sempai Malcolm. He was several inches taller than me and several stones heavier. He was also supremely fit and very heavily muscled. He fought in the heavyweight division. The prospect of being hit by him with full force did not bear thinking about, but thankfully he had great control and was always careful with us lower grades. This time, however, I was feeling a bit deranged. A bit hyped up about the tournament. So I decided to test myself against him.

As we sparred, I began putting in some harder punches and kicks. He sensed a new level of contact and matched it. I increased the level again, and slammed two more hard punches into his body. He hit back, hard, and caught me with a low kick, but I was able to withstand it. I increased the pressure again and launched another two-punch combination followed by a low kick to the inside of his thigh and another to the outside. This was about as hard as I could hit.

Gary paused for a moment and even gave me an appreciative nod. Then he smashed me with a two huge punches and slammed me into the wall. I gasped for breath. Pulling me forward, he threw his knee into my chest. I felt it touch, but no more. He'd pulled the strike at the last moment, leaving his knee up there for an extra second, as a reminder of what might have happened. I dreaded to think. Still, I was pleased that I had taken him to such a level.

A week before the tournament, I began dieting. I had to. I'd entered the lightweight division, which was anything up to 11 stone. But with all the weight training I'd done, I'd put on a fair bit of muscle. I was feeling strong and fit as a fiddle, but my natural weight was now 11 stone 10 pounds. This put me in a difficult position. I was still too light for a middleweight, but too heavy for a lightweight. I needed to add a few pounds and fight middleweight, or lose a few pounds and get down to 11 stone.

I decided I was too small to compete at middleweight. I would return to the relative safety of the lightweight division. At the last tournament, I'd shed a few pounds to reach 11 stone quite easily. This time the weight was proving harder to shift. Four days before the tournament, I still had six pounds to lose. I crash-dieted. I skipped meals. After a long, hard class I munched miserably on an apple.

The day before the tournament, the squad drove up to Oldham in a minibus. There was a weigh-in that evening, so I didn't eat or drink the whole day. When I got there, tired and drained, I weighed in at exactly 11 stone. Now that I'd made the weight, I could eat again. We were staying in a hotel near the sports arena, and had dinner in the restaurant. I tried to pile in as many calories as I could, but my stomach had shrunk. I was nervous. I couldn't fit much inside. The lads laughed and joked around the table, but we all knew what was in store the next day. It was gallows humour.

After a fitful night's sleep, I packed and repacked my bag, making sure I had everything I would need for a successful tournament. Water, food, shin pads, groin guard, life insurance. It felt good to be with the rest of the team. We supported each other and Sempai Malcolm was there as our coach.

When we got to the arena, I was keen to get on with it. Then came the worst part. The waiting. It was horrendous. Butterflies were going crazy in my stomach. I eyed the other fighters nervously. Who would I have to fight? Who's he? Who's that? Isn't he a champion? Is he lightweight? It was hard to tell. Everyone seemed so big, so much bigger than me.

This was another so-called regional tournament, but I noticed all the familiar faces from the nationals, plus fighters from abroad. I also noticed my old adversary, from the previous tournament. To my relief, he was fighting as a middleweight. I wasn't the only one who'd been eating too many pies.

I bounced around to warm up. I stretched. My body felt strong and supple. The adrenaline was helping my limbs to perform for me. I paced around anxiously, shadow boxing occasionally to release the tension. Eventually my name was called and I saw who I would be fighting. He wore a green belt, like me. Good. I had a reasonable chance of winning.

As I prepared to go onto the mat, Sempai Malcolm warned me not to underestimate him. He knew him. The guy was a regular on the tournament circuit. It's not uncommon for fighters to stay on green belt for many years and concentrate on tournaments rather than gradings. There's a form of reverse snobbery involved in beating brown and black belts when you're still a green belt. Was that his game?

He didn't look too dangerous. I prepared to step onto the mat with him. He looked strong, but quite unassuming. I decided I should be able to beat him and prepared to outsmart and outclass him. I was determined to get myself through to the later rounds this time.

The ten steps from the edge of the mat to the centre were some of the most arduous I've ever had to take. What was it about tournaments that made them so nerve-racking? It would take me a lot longer to truly understand. Walking then on watery legs, barely able to stop them shaking, I did my best to affect an air of nonchalance. I shut out the noisy crowd and kept my mind on the business of fighting. There was this guy in front of me, who was about to try and tear me apart. The only way to avoid it was to do it to him first.

The referee called us together, we bowed, just a short, sharp nod to each other, and then we began. I shouted loudly and stepped forward strongly. My opponent seemed less intense about the whole thing. I launched several fast combinations and caught him with some good shots. He seemed slow in comparison and his punches had no effect on me. He wasn't a kicker. You can tell if someone has the flexibility to kick high. He didn't seem to have dangerous legs.

We fought hard for the next two minutes. I kept a relentless pressure on him, hitting and moving skilfully. He caught me a few times, but nothing troubled me. After two minutes, the referee stopped the round and conferred with the corner judges. I felt I was slightly ahead, but no one has done enough to win. We squared up for another round. I was pleased. This fight had already gone on longer than my previous one.

But I felt very drained. There didn't seem to be much left in the tank. I put this worry aside. When we began again, I relaunched my assault and kept him under pressure for the next minute, hitting him with everything I had. He seemed to have no answer. His shots didn't seem to be getting through. I hit him again and again, until my arms were so tired I could barely lift them. I was completely exhausted. I found myself gasping for air. In a moment of despair, I realised my frantic work rate had backfired on me. I had nothing left.

My opponent was canny enough to see I was out of gas, and launched his first real hard counterattack. He caught me with three or four hard hooks into the ribs. Normally I could have taken these shots quite happily. Now, with no air in my lungs, they were hurting like hell. I backed away but he stayed right on top of me, hooking hard shots into my ribs until I hunched over to protect them. My head went down, and it was a fatal error. With perfect timing, his knee came up the middle and connected with my face.

Then I hear someone calling from far away:

'Hello?'

'What?'

'Hello!'

The ref was kneeling in front me. What's he doing there, I wondered. And why is he slapping me in the face? Why am I sitting on the floor?

Slowly, I pieced together what happened. I'd been knocked out.

I'd only been unconscious for a split second, but it took a while for my memory to return. The ref checked my face. I had a nasty cut on my lip. He tested my vision and made sure I knew who I was. Then he helped me to my feet, so I could take the formal bow. As I was leaving the mat, he ordered me over to the medics for a more thorough check up.

They did a few basic tests and told me to take it easy for a week or two. I got changed, forlornly. I was angry with myself for fighting naively. I'd made a stupid mistake, again, and lost. I'd blown myself out trying to get a knockout against a tough opponent. I should have had the confidence to pick my moments. I needed to find openings first, and then attack hard. I still had a lot to learn about strategy.

This loss affected me more than my previous one, because I felt I'd had a good chance of winning. However, my opponent did end up with a bronze medal, which showed he knew what he was doing. My crash dieting had left me feeling very weak, and I realised I needed to take more care of my weight.

In the weeks that followed, I felt disillusioned with karate. I knew if I entered a few more tournaments, I'd eventually learn the ropes. I'd stop making naive errors and might even win some medals. But I also knew I would never be a great champion. There were some guys that had a natural gift for fighting, and loved the thrill of competition. I was not one of them.

I simply accepted tournaments as a valuable training aid and a good test. They put you under a level of pressure that simply can't be achieved under normal conditions. Nothing makes you train harder than a knockdown fight. And nothing gives you quite as much confidence once you've come out the other end (even if your face is a bit of a mess).

I wasn't looking forward to going home. My girlfriend had decided not to come and watch me this time. Karate was too violent. *'Stupid boys' games'*, she'd call it, when she was in a mood to tell me what she thought. Maybe she was right.

By the time I got home late at night, an oozing scab had formed across my top lip. It was so long, it was practically a moustache. She demanded to know what *that thing* was on my face. I told her it was a mat burn. (Nylon mats can give you a nasty friction burn.) She knew I was telling porkies.

'Did you win?' She demanded.

'No, I lost,' I admitted.

'What happened? Did he wipe the floor with your face?'

I was too crap at lying to keep it hidden from her. I admitted I'd been knocked out. She was disgusted with me.

'Why didn't you keep your hands up, you twat?'

Not really. But she did think I was insane. She couldn't understand why I'd put my health in such jeopardy. She never asked me to quit, because she knew how much karate meant to me, but her opinion was set from then on.

On Monday morning, I was deeply embarrassed by my scab. I knew there'd be no hiding it at work. I left Oxford Circus underground and walked miserably up Great Portland Street. All too soon, I was passing the chairman's Bentley and the long, elegant BMWs that belonged to the directors. Then I was at the entrance. The doorman greeted me with a smile. I murmured a quick hello and hurried past, before he could quiz me about my face.

But in the office, under the harsh glare of the fluorescent strip lights, there was no hiding it. Most of my colleagues were women. One by one their faces changed from inquisitive: *What's that on your face?* to horrified: *Gosh, that must have hurt!* to embarrassed: *What a twat, he got knocked out.*

We gathered for our Monday morning meeting. I was late, as usual, and the boss was waiting impatiently. We went into his office and sat around his desk. He was wearing his little round designer glasses and making notes in his brand new 'desk-fax'. It was like a Filofax, only bigger and more expensive. He reached inside his jacket for his Mont Blanc pen, making sure we all saw the Armani label. Like I said, it was the eighties.

After the meeting, he kept me back and asked what was up with my face. I told him. He rolled his eyes, as if to say 'What the fuck are you doing?' I could understand his frustration. We were working in a high-pay, high-risk environment. Everyone was vying for favour with the chairman. There was a lot of politics and back-biting. Image was important. Perception was important. Every meeting was a performance of sorts and we needed to look and act the part. We had to be professional, or at least pretend to be.

I didn't give a damn about any of it and it showed. I got several more friendly warnings from my boss, and from my poor friend Tania, who'd got me the job in the first place. She must have been kicking herself. But I couldn't bring myself to care. I was amazed by most of the directors there. How could such people be in such highly paid jobs? They were so arrogant. So vain. Their greed and pettiness appalled me.

The only exception was my own boss. I liked him from the start. Yes, he was a 'yuppie', but he was also intelligent and dedicated and I learned a lot from him. He had a good sense of humour and knew how to have a good lunch. I think my attitude exasperated him, and eventually, quite understandably, his patience ran out. He gave me plenty of signs, but I still didn't see it coming. When he fired me, it hit me like a bolt from the blue, and hurt more than any punch or kick ever had.

I was stunned. Struck dumb. I argued back indignantly, feebly, lamely. Deep down, I knew he was right. I wasn't cut out for this type of work. I just couldn't believe it was happening to me. My first proper job and I got fired. What the heck was I going to tell my mother?

It took another two years before I got a job that I really wanted. Marketing had given me a glimpse of a job I knew I would love. A job I knew I could do very well, if someone gave me a chance. I wanted to be a writer. An advertising copywriter, to be exact.

I had no experience and no credentials. I taught myself from scratch. I read every book I could lay my hands on. I practised coming up with ideas every evening. I pestered professional copywriters until they agreed to critique my work. I listened to their advice and went back with new ideas, until I got the hang of it.

After two gruelling years and countless rejections, one agency boss finally offered me a two week trial. I didn't disappoint him. Two weeks later, a new phone list came around and my name was on it. My job description was 'copywriter'. It was an incredible moment for me.

I could breathe a huge sigh of relief. I had finally found a job I could care about. Work I could enjoy. I was thrilled. It seemed too good to be true. They were paying me to do something that was so much fun. I loved my job. And I still do. I just hope my clients don't read this, or they'll ask me to lower my fees.

The Wilderness Months

While I'd been working hard to get my career and my life back on track, I got used to training either alone or with Roy. I stayed away from the karate club. I held it partly responsible for my troubles, although in hindsight this was unfair.

In terms of training, I entered what I like to call my *Wilderness Months*. Roy and I trained together, unguided. We were free to do whatever we liked and for a while, it felt good. There was no pressure. No Sensei, no tournaments, no punishing fitness routines.

I cut out all the things I considered boring or unnecessary. No basic training (*kihon*) and no kata. I thought their purpose was ceremonial rather than practical. I concentrated on building up my power through bag work and weight training. But something curious happened. The longer I trained like this, the worse I became. I could barely hit the bag for 30 seconds before I tightened up. Something was wrong.

Eventually I realised that basics (*kihon*) was an important part of developing power. Sure, it only involved punching the air, but it served to loosen and stretch the body, developing an easy punching action. Alone, it is not enough to create a truly powerful punch, but combined with strength work, like press-ups, and bag work, it all added up to a better technique.

It became clear that Roy and I were floundering on our own. We were running out of ideas and making mistakes. We were strong and able fighters, but we still had little understanding of what we were doing. This must have been obvious to everyone and one evening at the gym, the resident taekwondo instructor took pity on us and invited us into his class.

I had little interest in taekwondo. Though similar to karate, with white suits and belts, it is a Korean art and specialises in high kicks, which was never my forte. It seemed a little light compared to my previous training, but I accepted his invitation, mainly out of courtesy. His name was Stav, and to my shame, I never found out his second name.

I went to the first class in a tracksuit instead of a traditional white *gi*. I was just trying it out. The warm-up was light and fast and they did a lot of stretching and kicking. Stav spent some time with me, working on my technique. He told me to relax and kick more naturally, with less effort. Try as I might, I couldn't to do what he wanted. I felt frustrated and a little annoyed. So what if I couldn't kick like them? I knew I was stronger and tougher than any of his students.

The lesson was less intense than Kyokushinkai. Stav was a third dan instructor and far more approachable than Sensei had been. He stopped to explain things during class, so we got an occasional breather. I learned later that he was a financial adviser in real life. He definitely had the gift of the gab.

Towards the end of the lesson, we did a little sparring. Most of his students were very flexible and had nice high kicks, but I knew I could flatten them if I wanted to. They had never hit, or been hit, as hard as I had.

Next week, I was in two minds whether to go again. But it was quite relaxing and enjoyable, so I decided to train a few more times.

A week or two later, two of Stav's mates paid a visit to the club. I'd seen them before; they were from a hard school of kung fu called Wu Shu Kwan. It was one of the few martial arts that entered Kyokushinkai tournaments and did well, instead of getting a pasting.

After a warm-up, Stav dedicated most of the lesson to sparring. I'd been to enough classes for Stav to know that I was a respectful student, with good self-control. So this time, he decided to spar with me himself. I wondered how good he'd be. He was small and light, and must have been in his late thirties. I was unsure what to expect. As I stepped forward to close the distance on him, something blocked my way. I'd walked straight onto a side kick. I hadn't even seen it. Just felt it.

It took me a moment to regain my composure. So... he was fast. I got up onto my toes to see if I could match him. I'd done some touch-fighting too. But my opponents had been amateurs in comparison. I'd never experienced anything like this. Each time I moved, I got caught. A kick in the belly... in the ribs... a punch to the chest... a spinning back kick, a front kick, a turning kick... he was going through the whole bloody syllabus!

I covered up to protect my body and his foot sailed over my guard and brushed past my face. He was picking me off at will. Frustrated, I piled into him, and tried to fight in close, using hooks, uppercuts and knees. He told me to back off. He knew I could fight like this, but that was not what he was teaching. And he was right. If I was in a taekwondo class, I had to spar by taekwondo rules.

When we changed partners, I found myself facing Burt, one of the guys from Wu Shu Kwan. He was tall and rangy, with long, powerful legs. As we began, he shifted his weight onto his back foot and stood poised, still as a statue. I was bemused. I stepped in with a turning kick but his front leg lashed out and caught me first, knocking me onto my arse.

I got up and brushed myself down with all the dignity I could muster. I prepared to fight with a bit more intensity. I bounced in and out, just out of range, then lunged forward with a punch. Before I got anywhere near him, there was something blocking my vision. His foot was hovering half an inch from my face. I backed off, thankful for his control.

His legs were so long that I had no chance of getting past them. I knew I'd have to use slip-timing. I needed to get him to kick first, then attack as he was drawing his leg back. I could think of no other way of getting in. I dummied forward, once, to draw his kick, but he wasn't fooled. I dummied again, this time a little further, a little *too* far, because his foot hovered an inch from my face again. So much for tactics. I held my hands high and piled into him. I was resorting to a style that was *not* what we were supposed to be practising. I was being crude, and I think Burt felt a little pity for me. He pushed me away nonchalantly.

We changed partners and I fought Burt's friend, Anthony. He was more laid back, but again, I seemed to walk onto something each time I moved. His timing was immaculate. I got frustrated. His kicks were not particularly fast or aggressive. They simply caught me when I wasn't expecting them. As I moved forward, I got hit. As I dropped my hand, I got hit in the head. As I covered my head, I took one to the body. I had no answers.

These guys were all experienced black belts, and it was clear they were playing with me. Not one kick had been too hard, but the thought had been there. How many times could they have taken my head off that night?

And how could Stav be *so fast?* I began to wonder if it his speed was something you could learn. I'd only come across it once before. One guy at the Kyokushinkai seemed to have that form of blinding speed. I'd assumed it was just something he was born with. A gift from God. Now I noticed that Stav seemed to move the same way. Maybe there was a knack to it?

I was intrigued. Could I learn it too? I joined the club officially and decided to invest some time in finding out. I imagined how good it would be to add such speed to my armoury. Sadly, Roy was not so interested, and didn't turn up very often. We still trained together for a while, but eventually we lost touch.

I got myself a taekwondo licence and found myself reduced to white belt all over again. But although I stood with the lower grades, Stav still treated me as one of the seniors. He spent time with me before the lessons, working on my technique. '*Relax*,' he'd say. I thought I was relaxed. '*More* relaxed,' he'd say. I tried. I seemed to be getting nowhere.

I watched Stav carefully, all the time, to see how he did it. I tried to mimic his movements. One night, he was preparing two of his senior students for a grading. They needed to break a wooden board and he wanted to give them some practice. He asked me to hold a pad for them. I clutched it against my shoulder and they began striking it with the inside ridge of their palms. Both were big strong boys, perhaps 13 stone apiece, but they weren't making much impression on the pad.

Stav told them to stop swinging their arm in isolation, but rather whip their whole bodies around explosively and connect with the hand at the last instance. He demonstrated. I watched as he stood in front of me, preparing to strike. His feet were evenly placed and he bounced almost imperceptibly, as if trying to get in touch with his bodyweight (which for the record, can't have been much more than ten stone). Then there was blur and a loud 'crack'. I felt a sharp pain in my shoulder. His strike had gone right through the pad and into me. It felt twice as hard. And it was pure technique.

The guys also needed to break tiles which would be resting on bricks close to the floor. To practise, Stav put two pads on the floor and rested a third on top. He told them to hit the pad. They bent over and dropped big punches onto it. He was not happy.

'Stop punching with your arms and hands,' he pleaded. 'Hit with your whole body!'

He stood in front of the pads, perfectly straight. I noticed him relax his back and shoulders, then rise up onto his toes and hover for a moment, drawing breath. Then he vanished. Another loud crack echoed around the hall as his fist connected with the pad.

He seemed to be able to collapse his body at will. There was no resistance on the way down. No stiffness. He could drop his whole self like a stone. How did he manage it? I began to watch him even more closely, really observing his movements. He spent a lot of time stretching, loosening his muscles, shaking his limbs until they seemed to be made of jelly.

'Relax,' he kept telling me. 'Breathe,' he'd remind me. My inability to move like him was frustrating me, making me even more tense. My progress was slow. Until, after several months of getting nowhere, something happened.

A kick snapped out and back very fast, very relaxed. It felt just right. To my delight, Stav noticed straight away.

'That's the best you've ever done,' he told me, happy that his perseverance was finally paying off. I knew I was onto something. I was getting the knack. At last, I'd taught my body to relax. I applied the same principle to all other kicks and my punches, blocks and strikes. I began to understand the *physics* that was at work, and why relaxation was as important as strength.

Throwing a good punch works like firing a gun. Once the explosion has taken place in the barrel, the bullet flies of its own accord. It accelerates naturally. It doesn't need to be pushed along. A good punch is the same. An explosive body movement launches the punch. It starts in the legs and hips, travels through the torso and into the shoulder. The arm is the last part to move. Once the fist is travelling, there's no need to push it along. Engaging the arm muscles will simply retard the motion. The muscles need to relax and simply allow the fist to fly home.

I realised it was the same for all movement. Before we take a step, we sink our weight. The leg bends, then straightens. The faster we sink, the faster we rise. The fastest way to sink is not to lower yourself with your leg muscles. It is to relax completely. This split-second collapse triggers an explosive reply from the legs to prevent you falling over completely, which leads to a faster, more explosive step forward.

It's just physics. What's often called 'body mechanics'. But understanding the theory doesn't mean you can make it work for your body. That only comes from long hours of practice. Still, it was rewarding. I was beginning to understand the principles of martial arts. Once you understand principles, everything else falls into place.

I had Stav to thank for that. But although I learned a lot from him, I was never very comfortable with taekwondo. Deep down, I knew it wasn't for me. I admired the skill and beauty of their kicks and their lightning speed. I was glad I'd added a little of this to my arsenal, but in the long term, I couldn't see myself staying there. I trained for about two years in total, until fate (or perhaps it was the Tao) moved me in a new and different direction.

Curtain Road

I loved my new job as a writer. The agency would have made a great setting for a sitcom. The bosses were unashamed slave drivers. They thought nothing of briefing us at five-thirty and asking for ideas by nine-thirty the next morning. We regularly worked all night.

I enjoyed every minute of it. There was always a great atmosphere in the Creative Department. After a long night's work we'd order in pizza or curry and a few beers. The company paid for cabs to take us home. In the small hours the roads around London were deserted. We'd drive across Westminster Bridge and get a great view of the Houses of Parliament lit up at night.

After two years of this hectic existence, I got myself a cushier number in an elegant financial agency in the City. The pay was better and the hours less punishing. I even had time for lunch once in a while. On the long summer evenings, we'd play bowls on the lawn in Finsbury Square. I was practically a City gentleman, minus the pinstripe suit.

Meanwhile, the taekwondo classes had been suspended. There was some problem with the gym and we were told to await news of reopening. I decided this was my cue to quit the club, without facing up to the difficult task of telling my instructor I was leaving.

Though I'd learned some amazing lessons from Stav, and had been inspired by him, I knew taekwondo was not for me. I was not a natural kicker and never would be. To my shame, I slunk off without ever saying goodbye or thank you. In writing this I have tried to trace Stav on the internet, or at least find his surname, without success. Stav, if you're reading this: I apologise. I hope the dedication at the front of this book will make up for my rudeness.

I couldn't imagine life without some sort of martial arts. It was in my blood now, part of who I was. I decided to go back to my first love: karate. But which club? Which style? I checked the Yellow Pages and found there was a dojo around the corner from my work. They practised a well-known style which I'd not tried before. Kyokushinkai had been influenced by it. It was Goju Ryu, which translates literally as *hard-soft school*.

The instructor was a sixth dan master who was well-known in the UK. He had written many long and learned articles in the karate press, and had excellent credentials. I phoned to find out more and spoke to Shihan Chris Rowen. It was a strange conversation. Many of my preconceptions about karate were challenged immediately.

I asked him which nights the club was open. 'Every night,' he answered, as if puzzled by the question. The club was also open at lunchtime. 'It's a full-time dojo,' he explained. 'There's also training in the morning, if you want it.'

This was interesting. Unusual. I decided to go and find out more. At lunchtime the next day, I headed out of Finsbury Square and around the corner to Curtain Road. Next to a bar called the Paper Mill was a doorway with a wooden sign and Japanese calligraphy. I assumed it must be the dojo.

I went up some stairs. There was a sign requesting for all visitors to take off their shoes. Several pairs were already arranged on a shoe rack outside the door. I put mine with the others, wondering what we'd do if a desperate thief came along and stole the whole lot.

Inside, there was a glass-fronted office. Chris was inside. I introduced myself as politely as I could. He gave me a form to complete and took a few minutes to tell me about his background and the dojo. I discovered he had trained in the Tokyo headquarters of Goju Ryu under the famous grandmaster Gogen Yamaguchi. Chris's master grade had been awarded directly from Tokyo. He stressed that he modelled his training on the way things were run in Japan in the old days. He had a very traditional outlook.

The dojo was impressive. There was an expanse of polished wooden flooring and a wall of mirrors. A punch bag hung in a corner, and two wooden striking posts were fitted against the wall. These were traditional makiwara, used to condition the knuckles of the fist for punching. At the front was an attractive shrine, complete with old black and white photos of two famous masters, Yamaguchi and Miyagi. (Not Mr Miyagi from *The Karate Kid*, this was Miyagi Chojun, the founder of Goju Ryu.)

I was intrigued to try this new style of karate and attended regularly; lunchtimes and evenings. Shihan Chris often took the sessions, and I noticed a very different approach to training. A different mindset. He frowned on competitions and believed training should always be geared towards a real 'life-or-death' encounter. The way he taught reflected this. There were no pads or gloves. We practised striking to the face or neck, and kicking to the knee joints, groin or pelvis.

There were no high kicks. All kicks were aimed below the belt. I'd read about this in magazines. In older, more traditional styles of kung fu and karate, high kicks were considered impractical for real fighting. I could see why. First, you need to be naturally supple, because there's no time to warm up and stretch. And second, unless you know what you're doing, high kicks can put you off balance and make you vulnerable. If your leg is caught, you're in a bad position.

That said, there are some people who *can* use high kicks effectively at the drop of the hat. Good luck to them, I say. I wasn't one of them. I was happy to practise these low-level kicks that could be used any time, anywhere.

We learned a variety of unusual strikes. Chris showed us new ways to hit using the fist, forearm, palm, edge of the hand or individual knuckles. There were 32 striking areas between the elbow and fingertips. Soon I was learning the first kata, which translates loosely as 'attack and smash'. Then one day, to my amazement, Chris took each move from the kata and showed us what it meant.

It may sound incredible, but in over ten years of training, no one had ever done that before. Other styles seemed to use kata as a drill to develop power and grace, or as a *nod* towards the traditional origins of their styles, but their main focus was always competition. Here, the katas were not kept alive out of respect for the past. They were real working models.

We practised attack and defence from the kata with partners. Things began to fall into place. For many years, I'd read that kata was at the heart of karate. The secrets of karate were contained in the kata. I'd never understood how or why. It had been an enjoyable exercise. But I'd always felt sparring was at the heart of a fighting system. Now I was beginning to change my view.

I leaned how each kata was a collection of prearranged answers to an attack: what to do if someone tries to punch you in the face... grab you by the wrist... take you by the lapels... kick you in the groin... Each kata had a new set of answers. Some were very direct, a simple parry and counter strike followed by a throw. Others were more fluid, using circular motion to redirect the opponent's power. We practised the attack and defence drills over and over again, until they became second nature. This was called *bunkai*: the *applications* of the kata.

I began to appreciate the beauty of the kata. It is a wonderful physical record of a set of self-defence moves. It was quite poetic. The individual blocks and punches were like words. The two-step block and strike combinations were phrases. The whole kata was like a poem created by a master. A set of disparate moves collected into a simple, elegant piece that was easy to remember and practise on your own. When the kata was performed by a master, it was both powerful and graceful, poetry in motion.

The *bunkai* were far more pragmatic. If you weren't careful, you were liable to get a smack in the mush. We would begin from a safe distance and then step closer, almost face to face, before starting. Chris emphasised that real fighting was always close range; 'up close and personal', he liked to describe it. There's no time to get into a fighting stance and no space to dance around your assailant. He's right there, in your face. Now what do you do?

The reasoning made sense, but I was uncomfortable being so close. We would stand square, an arm's length apart, our hands by our sides. Then we would practise blocking a punch in a circular motion and gripping the wrist. We learned to control the arm and pull the opponent into a bad position, or onto a counter attack. After a while, I got used to operating at this new range.

Chris gave me keys to the dojo, so I could train whenever I wished. At lunchtimes there were usually only three or four people training and we'd spend an enjoyable hour drilling kata and bunkai over and over.

If my friend Adrian was there, we would often spar for the best part of an hour. We were the same grade and he'd also done other styles before. We mixed some touch-fighting techniques with some of the new Goju techniques we were learning, and developed a fast flowing style where anything was a target (except the eyes). Our contact was light to medium, with the emphasis on fluidity and combinations.

Soon we got to know each other's style so well that we cancelled each other out. Neither could land a technique on the other, unless we came up with a new move. This meant we had to be creative.

One lunchtime, during a typical sparring match, Adrian launched a big looping right hander to the side of my head. It was one of his specialities, and he did it very well. I saw it coming a mile off and raised my left hand to block. Suddenly a front kick caught me completely unawares. The punch had been a feint.

So the boy had a new move. I'd have to be wary. To my annoyance, he caught me many more times with the same trick. Though I knew it was a trap, I fell for it every time. My muscle memory was programmed to react to the looping right hand by raising my left. Now I had to deprogramme this, because he was using it against me. Many front kicks later, I succeeded. And it worked better than I could have ever hoped.

As his looping right hand shot out, I stepped forward and thrust my left arm forward, inside the arc of his punch. When his arm hit mine, it knocked my palm into the side of his own face. It was one of those rare, perfect techniques that you read about. A Zen moment. My opponent's force had been redirected and used against him, with very little effort. It felt great. I wanted to experience it again, but it never worked quite as well again.

What I enjoyed most about our sparring was the creative atmosphere. We fought fast and friendly. We were competitive, but playful. We allowed each other to experiment. Mistakes were not punished, they were just mocked. There was no ego.

Once in a while we would increase the level of contact. Being heavier than Adrian, I was able to drive him back with hard body shots and low kicks onto the thighs, which he wasn't used to. But when I got carried away and cornered him, catching him with a barrage of punches, he got annoyed and smashed me in the mouth. It was hard enough to loosen the crown on my front tooth. I was a bit more wary after that. A new crown ain't cheap.

One lunchtime, we were the only two training. We were practising *bunkai* attack and defence sequences, over and over.

We chatted in between, enjoying the relaxed atmosphere. We didn't hear Shihan Chris come in. He came over. We stopped. He asked us to continue. Then he stood and watched, his weight on one foot, stroking his chin and frowning over the top of his glasses. After a minute, he stopped us.

'This time,' he told to me, 'really try to hit him in the face as hard as you can.'

Well, it *was* Adrian, and he did deserve it for loosening my tooth. I stepped forward strongly and threw my fist hard into his face. He blocked quickly, narrowly avoiding a bloody nose.

'Harder,' said Chris.

I lunged forward with a loud '*kiai*' and threw another punch right into Adrian's face. He was now on full alert and made sure his block was perfectly timed. Again, my fist sailed over his head at the last instance.

'This is how you should attack and defend every time,' Chris explained. 'You must act with *intent*. You must really mean everything you do. It's not a game. Make it your mindset at all times.'

A few days later there was a short curtain hanging over the entrance to the dojo. It covered the upper half of the doorway. It was made of thin black cloth, with Japanese embroidery. Did it signify something? Was there no training today? Was it some kind of special occasion? I looked for a sign or notice, but there was no clue to the curtain. Bemused, I ducked under it and began to warm up.

Soon the class filled up and others came in, equally bewildered by the curtain. Eventually Chris entered the dojo and the class began. Half way through, he paused and began to talk about one of his favourite themes: awareness. We listened. But as usual, didn't hear.

'How many of you noticed a curtain when you came in?' he asked.

Most people put their hands up, though not everyone, believe it or not.

'So, how did you enter the dojo?' he asked.

'Ducked under,' I muttered. 'Pushed it to one side,' others said. 'Can't remember,' said one. (There's no hope for some people, is there?)

'Who noticed it was actually two curtains, joined in the middle?' he asked.

No one answered. No one had. Chris stepped behind the curtain and demonstrated the correct way to enter. He slid both hand through the gap, pushed each curtain to the side and stepped strongly through the centre.

I realised this simple demonstration was a metaphor for something much more subtle. As Chris spoke, I began to understand what he was trying to get across. He explained how, in feudal Japan, the Samurai was always on his guard. Each new room could contain an enemy and needed to be entered with caution. *Awareness*. It would be unseemly for a Samurai to peep around corners, or enter half-heartedly, appearing to be nervous or afraid. If someone was waiting to attack him, the Samurai wanted to be up and ready to engage them.

So the Samurai would always be alert. His eyes would pick up subtle changes (like a new curtain), his ears would hear any unusual sounds. He would step into a new room correctly, in a state of readiness, not arse-first as I had.

This was one of my favourite and most memorable moments in karate. Thank you, Shihan Chris, for your simple and wonderful demonstration of 'Zanshin' (awareness). As you can see, it has stayed with me ever since.

I began to understand the significance of bowing on the way into the dojo. It was something I'd done automatically, for many years, without thinking. But the curtain taught me the purpose of the action: to be aware of your surroundings. To focus the mind firmly in the present, the here and now, to be fully prepared for your training. When you're practising dangerous techniques, you need to concentrate. If you don't, people are liable to get hurt.

At Chris's dojo, we would also bow to the shrine and the photos of the old masters. This was a mark of respect to the people who made the training possible for us. They had been through the same trials and tribulations we had. Their efforts in the past meant we could enjoy karate today. We bowed to our instructor and fellow students for the same reason. We all needed each other to train.

Perhaps the most interesting bow is on the way out of the dojo. Clocking out, instead of clocking in. It's arguably the most important moment of all. Despite what you might think, you're leaving the safety of the dojo for a far more dangerous place. The outside world. The bow can serve as a reminder to carry awareness with you when you leave. It will serve you well, especially if you're walking home late at night, or unlocking your car in a dark car park. There is no need to be fearful. But it is important to be aware.

These days when I come home and unlock the door, I listen and look. This is not paranoia. It's just living in London. A few years ago I disturbed burglars when I got home. They left through the window before I saw them, and they took nothing, but the possibility of it happening again is always there. I know two people who have woken up to find burglars *in the house*. Similarly, when walking home in the dark, I keep my eyes and ears open and avoid daydreaming.

If you go on a self-defence course with an instructor who knows what they're talking about, they'll tell you awareness is your most powerful weapon. Carry it with you at all times. It will help you spot trouble in advance and avoid it, instead of stumbling blindly into it. If trouble is inevitable, then at least you've had some warning and some time to prepare yourself.

Awareness is also vital in fighting. At tournaments, I had already paid the price for momentary lapses in concentration. It's the unexpected attack that does the most damage. The punch you don't see coming. During fighting, your awareness needs to burn like a bright spotlight, bringing all that's happening into sharp focus. You need to see the attacks coming, spot openings, avoid errors and punish mistakes. After a while, your ability to process all this information increases. You upgrade your chip. Eventually you can predict the future. A movement in the shoulder means a punch is coming, which will leave an opening for you to hit.

Occasionally we were allowed to spar. But Chris did not really approve. It was too close to playing as far as he was concerned. Even when we did spar, it was nothing like I'd done before. We would attack the face, neck, groin, joints; all the places I'd never been allowed to aim for before. Any target was allowed, but naturally, the level of contact was very light. Still, we were learning to target vulnerable points. This brought a new level of seriousness and responsibility to the sparring. We had to have faith in each other.

Chris would get us to stand face to face, at arm's length, and fight without moving our feet. It was very disconcerting. I couldn't pull back or step aside. At first we would strike at each other's faces with our eyes almost shut, due to the worry of getting hit. It's almost impossible not to blink. But after a while we got the hang of it and began to relax. With a good opponent, you could get into a rhythm and learn to parry almost everything, while striking back at the openings.

One lunchtime, Chris decided to spar with each of us in turn. I was intrigued to see what would happen. Though I knew he had done some tournaments before, I wondered how good his sparring would be. He placed so little emphasis on it.

When my turn came, I stood in front of him, feet squarely planted, my guard held high. He was tall, over six foot, and had a longer reach than me. I began by venturing a few tentative punches, which he parried effortlessly, catching me at the same time with a whipping back fist to the temple or a ridge hand to the neck. I picked up the pace and began throwing faster combinations, but he continued to pick me off.

Finally, I decided to go all out and see what happened. I dummied and feinted with some jabs and crosses, then threw fast combinations. His hands sped up and I was still unable to get near him. Soon it all became a blur and I had no idea what was happening. Meanwhile, Chris was still perfectly in control.

Then, he increased the pace again. I couldn't follow. His punches and strikes rained down and around my head. Each time I moved to block one, the next came through the opening, flicking me on the nose or mouth, catching me on the ear, neck, temple, stomach. I punched back, hopelessly, and he began attacking my punches. When my arm went out, he smashed up under my forearm with his wrist, or cracked down on it with the heel of his hand.

I began to run out of ideas, and tense up. Now my strikes were even easier to stop. Each time I extended my arm, I felt him tap it gently with both palms, a clapping motion, one hand at my wrist, the other at my elbow. My joints felt a nasty twinge. I had the feeling he could break my arm quite easily, if he wanted. Then he switched to an upper and lower action, near my wrist. I felt he could snap my wrist at will. Finally, I could take no more, and turned away. Chris gave me a friendly kick up the arse and called out the next person.

I was suitably impressed and humbled. Again, I had been given a glimpse of true mastery in a certain type of fighting. Though his fighting style was almost the opposite of Stav's, I noticed similar principles at work. Chris had been very relaxed throughout. He had read everything I was throwing at him instantly and answering automatically, without thinking. He had simply accepted the openings I was offering and taken them.

The interesting thing was, he never moved his feet once. All this speed and power came from one stance. Was this 'Sanchin' that I had heard so much about? It was a key aspect of Goju. Once mastered, it enables you to generate great power from a stationary position. I had seen Stav get great speed and power by moving his whole body. But how did Chris get his without even moving his feet? I was fascinated, and determined to learn his methods.

I had been busted down to white belt yet again, because there was a whole new grading syllabus to learn. But I progressed quickly through the ranks and over the next few months, Chris took more interest in me. He would demonstrate close range strikes, moving his hand just a few inches and striking at the ribs or the side of the neck. These short blows were incredibly painful. How did he generate such power? I was in awe.

His first love was kata and he spoke of each one as if it had a personality. As I learned more katas, I began to understand. There were certain themes running through them. The early ones were simple but effective. They were mainly about kicking and punching. The more advanced kata also contained grappling techniques, throws and locks, plus strikes with other parts of the hand and arm.

People often talk of the kata containing secret or *hidden* techniques. Students and even some instructors practise kata without any idea what they really are. There is simply the promise that all will be revealed at a later date. In frustration, some instructors make up their own interpretations of these movements, with varying degrees of success.

Whether the 'real' techniques were hidden deliberately, or whether they are simply hard to see without an expert guide is still a matter of debate. But Chris was making sense of kata for me. I was learning how each one contained a vast array of nasty little strikes, grips, tears and gouges that all were extremely painful. As we got higher up the ranks, with more control, Chris began to unveil more dangerous techniques.

I discovered he was very well read, a scholar of the martial arts. He spoke fluent Japanese, and his office was basically a library of books. Sometimes he would pause during a lesson and simply talk to us for half an hour on strategy or philosophy. He would take a Japanese word or calligraphy symbol and start from there. His wonderful monologues sparked my interest and I decided to find out more about my art.

Training at the Worcester Judo Club in the mid-seventies

Training for the Thirty Man Kumite in Kilburn, 2002

Fighting under Senseis Dan Lewis (L) and Gavin Mulholland (R)

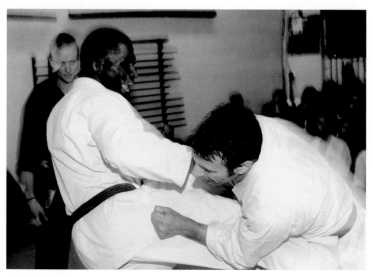

A vicious low kick from Tunde Oladimeji during fight 12

Exchanging punches with Oisin Carr, fight number 14

Fighting Andrew Bawden, 21st fight

Fight number 22 against Diccon Yamanaka

Last eight fighters including Mark Salomone
(4th from right) and Carl McKenzie (far right)

A knee goes in and gives me something to smile about

Fight number 29 against Paul Chapman

The final fight, number 30, against Carl McKenzie

At the end of the Thirty Man Kumite

A pint of Guinness with Sensei Gavin Mulholland

With Charmaigne in Kilburn, December 2002

Early on, I had read two famous books on strategy, *The Art of War* and *The Book of Five Rings*. Neither had made much sense to me. Now I reread them and things began to fall into place. I began to understand the strategy and tactics of the battlefield. I found I could relate them to my own experiences in karate.

Chris was also a Shinto priest and often spoke at length about life, morals, karate history, Zen… whatever took his fancy. I loved listening to these impromptu lectures. I felt I was being shown a glimpse of something fascinating that was out there for me to discover.

I began to read up on other subjects: Zen, Taoism, Buddhism. I was suddenly thirsty for knowledge. I read more martial arts books but was always disappointed with the explanations. Perhaps it was the translations? I wanted to learn about everything regarding strategy, fitness, diet, tactics, and above all, the mind. There was still one question that bothered me above all others.

Can you ever truly conquer fear?

Eventually, my research led me to a curious place. It was a big 'no-no' as far as karate was concerned and I kept it quiet from everyone, especially Chris. It was Western boxing.

Karate had always maintained a haughty superiority to boxing, on the basis that it uses more deadly techniques. Boxers are vulnerable to kicks. They are unused to fighting without gloves on, blah blah blah. At first, I bought into this theory, but still enjoyed watching matches on TV.

Then one day at work, early in my career, I'd found myself standing in the same room as Nigel Benn. He'd been visiting our firm on business, and was chatting to people in my office. Standing in his smart suit, talking and joking with his manager and their associates, there was still a strong sense of smouldering belligerence and power about him.

I'd been training hard for knockdown and was as strong and fit as I have ever been. We were roughly the same weight. I wondered how I would fair against him in a tear up. I didn't fancy my chances in the slightest. And when I watched more of his fights, I realised he was in a completely different league, like all the top professional boxers. Their levels of skill, fitness and power were off the scale, even compared to the best karate fighters I had seen.

This was not because boxing was innately better than karate or even because they were natural fighters and athletes, it was because they were full-time professionals, working many hours every day. They were conditioned to cope with levels of contact and punishment that most karate fighters could not even contemplate. Why? Because there was money and glory in boxing. Big money, for the fighters who were prepared to risk everything at the highest levels.

I had read classic karate texts and articles in magazines, but found nothing very realistic about mental attitude. All the great masters seemed to be fearless warriors. The older they were, the more legendary their feats. They had never lost a fight. They had defeated all challengers. Their power grew to mythological proportions. The further back in history you looked, the more zeros you could add to the number of people they had defeated.

Older and wiser, I was beginning to suspect it was a load of old bollocks, just part of the Eastern tradition of honouring the elderly, and especially the dead. No bad thing for sure, but not a very realistic basis for research.

When I read boxing books, I found them refreshingly free of bullshit. Fighters wrote openly about their hopes and fears, their triumphs and their losses. I took immediate comfort from the fact that some of the greatest boxers of all time felt nervous before a fight, just like I did. I wasn't alone.

I began spending many hours watching tapes of great fights and top fighters. I listened to interviews with the boxers and their coaches. My favourite was *When We Were Kings*, the award-winning documentary about the Rumble in the Jungle, Muhammad Ali's extraordinary win over George Foreman in Zaire. I watched it many times. It was fascinating.

Ali psyched himself up for months before the fight, visualising and verbalising his defeat of Foreman over and over. His plan was to dance around the younger, bigger, stronger Foreman. To dazzle him with his skill. But on the night, it was too hot to dance. The ring was soft and spongy and Ali was no longer a young man. So he changed his plan and surprised everyone by going toe-to-toe with Foreman and trying to knock him out. This only succeeded in enraging Foreman who, from round two onwards, had Ali on the ropes and hammered huge punches into him almost at will.

Ali switched to a seemingly suicidal new tactic of baiting Foreman and soaking up the punishment for several more rounds, until Foreman finally punched himself into exhaustion. Ali delivered a beautiful coup de grâce knockout in the eighth.

It was a feat of skill and seat-of-the-pants strategy that only a master like Ali could have performed. Though unconventional, dangerous (and not much use to the average fighter) it demonstrated an important point. A seemingly unbeatable force can be overcome, with the right methods, just as Sun Tzu says in his classic book *The Art of War*. I was inspired.

I continued my research with boxing biographies and autobiographies. I watched matches and studied tapes. Pretty soon, the truth began to dawn on me. *They all knew fear.*

I didn't have to delve too deep to find that all boxers had nerves before a fight. Even the most fearsome fighters confessed to this in their calmer moments, though it was usually after they had retired (for the last time) and were writing their memoirs. I watched amazing footage of the most fearsome boxer of our age, Mike Tyson, as a young man. He was crying on his coach's shoulder before an amateur bout (which he then went on to win).

So boxers had nerves. How did they cope with them? How did they seem to be so confident before the big fights? I got some insight from watching pre-fight press conferences. I noticed boxers rarely had a good word to say about their opponents.

Mostly they were downright insulting and fistfights were not uncommon. This animosity was not staged just to sell tickets. They really did seem to despise each other. It was strange, because after their fights, they often showed each other great respect. Beneath all the bravado, they often seemed to like and admire each other.

When Mike Tyson was going to fight Lennox Lewis, he said he would eat Lewis's children! There was pandemonium at the press conference. On the night of the fight, there was a wall of security guards in the ring to keep the fighters apart until the first bell. Of course, it made for great theatre. But after the fight, Tyson spoke quite sincerely of his respect for Lennox and even mentioned Lennox's mother. His mindset had changed completely.

I realised that to enter a boxing ring and risk 12 rounds of pain, damage and even death, they couldn't enter in a normal state of mind. If they approached the fight rationally they would lose. Boxers were deliberately building themselves up into a frenzy of hatred and loathing against their opponent. They replayed scenes over and over in their minds, beating the other guy with punches and knocking them down, again and again. This was the only way to enter the ring with real, deep-seated self-belief. Now I understood.

I noticed boxers broadly fell into two camps: the 'boxers' and the 'fighters'. The boxers were technically excellent, master tacticians. They would stay out of trouble and strike when their opponent was vulnerable.

The fighters were devastating hitters. They were usually the fearsome ones. The mere sight of them could strike terror into their opponents' hearts. They would come forward relentlessly and overpower their opponents with savage combinations and little regard for their own safety.

Each constructed scenarios to suit their style. The boxers would create 'bull and matador' scenarios. Ali promised to dance around Foreman, to make him look foolish. The fighters wouldn't say anything. Instead, they would brood menacingly, and get into fights at the weigh-ins. The boxers would bait the fighters. The fighters would make ominous threats to the boxers.

Of course, it all helped to sell tickets, but it was not all an act. They were giving themselves an outcome to believe in. It was not all that realistic. But the truth about the pain and danger they were facing was too awful to contemplate rationally. They pushed it aside with a more favourable scenario.

I noticed they tended to repeat the same story over and over like a mantra, to themselves, the journalists, the fans, and anyone else who would listen. Ali is famous for this. His way with words and vivid imagination made for some hilariously funny scenarios and vicious verbal attacks on his opponents.

I noticed how cocky some of the boxers were. Chris Eubank. Naseem Hamed. The posing, the posturing, the antics, the talk. It was constant. They were deliberately filling their heads with positive thoughts, pouring them into their mind as fast as they could, to keep the dark thoughts at bay.

This is a simple but effective method of mind control. Call it auto-suggestion or self-hypnosis if you like. You are suggesting an outcome to yourself, over and over, to keep other more negative thoughts from troubling you.

Now I began to see the close link in martial arts to Zen. If you try to practise Zen meditation, one of the first things you learn is how difficult it is to control your own mind. Thoughts come and go completely of their own accord. It is almost impossible for a novice to clear their mind for more than a few seconds, before a new thought bubbles to the surface.

Students begin Zen practise by closing off all outside stimuli. They find a quiet place in a room and sit with their eyes half closed. They begin breathing slowly and deeply and count their breaths from one to ten. They try to concentrate on nothing but breathing and counting, but it's almost impossible. After three or four breaths, another thought appears. Try it yourself if you haven't already. I guarantee you won't get to ten without thinking of something else.

Or try this: think of a number, any number, as long as it's not 16. (Now what number did you just think of?) We have very little control over our own minds, our thoughts and emotions. You can tell yourself not to be nervous before an exam, but will it do you any good? Now imagine you're coming face to face with a monster. Can you simply tell yourself not to be afraid?

We can't simply ban our own nervousness. We can't consciously tell our fears to vanish. Our minds don't work that way. But we *can* distract ourselves. We can keep our mind so filled with other thoughts that it doesn't have a chance to dwell on the negatives.

We can replay scenes of triumph over and over again. We can picture our opponent broken, on their knees, or flat on their backs. We can picture them as a small frightened child. We can recite mantras of power and domination. We can hum songs, over and over, to keep our minds upbeat and positive. We can imagine actually 'being' our opponent, feeling his own fear. Fearing you. All these are infinitely preferable to the truth.

I learned that basically, I was far too nice. I'd been entering tournaments as if they were a college debating society. I had to learn to seriously disrespect my opponent as a fighter (while still respecting them as a person). Full-contact fighting is a small war. It's not rational or logical. Perhaps it's not even right. But once you decide to take part, you can't afford to cling to a balanced set of morals. Now I had the theory. But my chance to test it would come a little later.

The time I spent training under master Chris Rowen was a time of enlightenment for me. I was learning so many advanced principles of karate. I was not as fit as before, but I kept up some fitness work at home and felt very healthy. Besides, I was in my early thirties, and my career was beginning to take off. I moved to another agency in Clerkenwell and won several awards for my work. I was offered a more senior role in the company. I had a position of responsibility. I began hiring and firing.

My girlfriend and I got married. When our first child was born, a boy, Chris announced it to the dojo. I was touched. There was a warm atmosphere about the place, and I felt at home.

When the rent went up, we needed to move to new premises. Chris found a new place and every member of the club came along at the weekend to help out. We lifted the sprung flooring and took it with us. Some of the guys spent days plumbing and rewiring and in no time at all, we had a brand new dojo every bit as good as the old one.

Training with Chris was intense, but never punishing. We didn't spend hours doing fitness work. Chris concentrated on technique, so it was easy to train at lunchtime and again in the evening. I left the sessions feeling energised, instead of knackered. I began to train whenever I got the chance and progressed quickly through the belts. After a few years, I was ready to take my black belt.

I knew the grading would be long and exhaustive, covering the entire syllabus. I knew what Shihan was looking for. Perfection. Nothing less. I was excited to finally go for a black belt, after so many years of training, and spent extra time practising in the back yard. Each evening I ran through everything I needed for my grading. It took 90 minutes just to complete the syllabus once.

I spent extra time on my kata. Normally, my aim was to create an impressive performance for anyone watching. But I knew

Chris was a stickler for detail and perfection. He would spot the slightest mistakes. I was going to have to practise a different way and sort out all the tiny details. Ever foot movement, every hand position had to be just right. The man was never satisfied.

I began practising the first kata, over and over, concentrating first on my feet, then my legs, my hips, my hands, my breathing, my eyes, and finally my overall composure. I would stay on each area until I felt it was right. And a strange thing occurred. I noticed an incredible change in my ability, almost overnight.

I wasn't the only one. People commented in the dojo. It was obvious to everyone. This attention to detail, to perfection, was really paying off. When I speeded up now, the flow of power in my kata seemed effortless rather than forced. I was amazed. Getting all the little things right was making a big difference.

Chris talked about the four stages of learning a kata. I was beginning to understand. The first stage was simply learning the movements. The second was to practise slowly and correctly, until it became natural. This he described as '*ju-ho*', which can be translated as 'softly'. The third was to perform the kata hard and fast, with as much power as possible. This was called *go-ho*, or 'hard'. This was what I'd always done, until recently. The final way was '*go-ju*', which means both hard and soft, combined. This was our ultimate goal. It linked back to what I had learned from Stav. The importance of relaxation as well as explosion.

One evening, Chris demonstrated a kata both soft and then hard-soft. During the soft kata, he performed each move at a medium pace, with complete relaxation. As he rose onto one leg and prepared to kick, I noticed a small, almost imperceptible wobble. He sunk his weight to steady himself, and for a brief moment, he was completely still. Then he let fly with a kick and continued.

When he performed the same kata in a hard-soft style, there was no sign of the wobble. I realised why. By doing the kata slowly first, he was exposing his own slight imperfections in balance and correcting them. His body was learning exactness and correctness. When he speeded up, his balance had been recalibrated. It was perfect. And awesome to watch.

If you always do katas hard and fast, you can hide imperfections with bluster and power. But this is simply papering over the cracks. Doing a kata more slowly, without tension, allows you to dwell on your weaknesses and correct them. Once you speed up again, your movements are much more natural and more effective.

This was a moment of enlightenment for me. I felt Chris had shared another secret of training with us. This relaxed form of training was revealing many things to me, about the natural flow of momentum that takes place in the body. I began to understand that this was the mysterious '*Chi*' that I'd read so much about ('*Ki*' in Japanese).

It had made no sense to me before. Was there really some sort of invisible energy source that we could tap into whenever we liked? Of course not. But there is your own energy. You can learn to maximise it. I began to see *Chi* as physics and body mechanics rolled into one. The perfect trajectory for a punch is the so-called meridian of *Chi*. If you are too tense, you restrict your own movement, interrupting the flow of *Chi*. *Chi* is not an external source of energy. It is the body's natural energy and momentum used to its best effect.

The mysteries of the martial arts were finally beginning to clear up. I started using this soft style of training to uncover more about natural momentum. I tried all my movements and katas this way to see where it took me. I discovered that what I'd call '*Chi*' can be present in any movement and help it flow easily on to the next movement, with the right technique.

I passed my black belt. But wrapping it around my waist did not feel particularly special. More like something I should have attended to years ago. Besides, I was too fascinated by what I had started to uncover in my own training to bother about the black belt. I was just at the beginning of an exciting new journey.

Over the next few years I graded again to second dan and then third dan and began teaching occasionally at lunchtime. It was an interesting experience, and an enlightening time. But it wasn't to last. Our club was in the Old Street area, not far from Hoxton, which was rapidly becoming the trendiest place to convert a loft in all of London. The rent doubled in a year and we had to move again.

This time, we couldn't afford nice large premises and began training in a small community hall. The numbers dwindled and slowly, the atmosphere began to wane. Shihan had other commitments and could not spend the time with us that he wanted. Eventually, and with much regret, I began to search for another club.

I decided to stay with the Goju style. I'd found a style that suited me. It had the right mixture of realistic fighting applications with a spiritual and artistic side that appealed to me. I had learned to appreciate the beauty of kata and enjoyed studying the classic Goju katas in depth.

A friend emailed me a list of other Goju clubs. I noticed one in central London and decided it would be interesting to pay it a visit. With my background in full contact, and my new-found skill in kata, I was confident I'd be fine. I was in for a rude awakening.

Sensei, Sempai

My second child was born in the summer; a girl this time. I would bring her into the garden in her little seat, so she could watch her brother and me trimming the bushes and watering the grass. When the two of them were tucked up in bed, I would practise my kata for an hour or so in the yard. At weekends we'd go shopping, visit friends, or walk around the nearby park. Sometimes I would go for a run or train at the gym, and it caused friction. My wife wanted me to stay and help with the kids.

I took a chance and gave up my full-time job to become a freelance writer. The risk paid off. I got work at several top agencies and was happier than before. If one went quiet, I would get work from another that was busy. The lifestyle really suited me. I enjoyed the lack of office politics and I liked moving around between places in fashionable Soho and Covent Garden. I still do.

My search for a new karate club took me to a dojo near Oxford Circus, an easy walk after work. I checked their website. They trained on Mondays and Thursdays. They practised Okinawan Goju, which was different from my Japanese version. I was intrigued. Okinawa was the home of karate. How would it feel to go back to the very roots of the art?

I decided to turn up unannounced. I went early and asked at reception for the karate club. They pointed me down a flight of stairs to the gym. Here they pointed me down another set of stairs. I descended into the very bowels of the building.

I found the training room and was surprised to see mats on the floor. I guessed the karate club shared the room with judo or jujitsu, who normally use mats. I popped my head around the door. There was a black belt inside, rearranging the mats. His belt was tattered and worn almost white. He'd been a black belt for a long time.

I guessed he was the instructor and asked if he was Gavin Mulholland. He said he was. I introduced myself and asked if I could train that evening. He said I'd be welcome and showed me where to get changed. Almost as an afterthought, he asked me what grade I was. I told him third dan.

He raised his eyebrows and told me in that case, I would be standing at the head of the line. I was a little surprised. I'd never been the highest grade before. I wasn't keen to join a brand new class in such a conspicuous position. I told him, modestly, that I'd be happy to stand anywhere. He insisted I should stand at the front. I was flattered, but I knew this courtesy was a double-edged sword. All eyes would be on me from the very beginning. I wondered whether a few noses would be out of joint too.

I got changed and rejoined him in the dojo. We talked for a while about karate. He seemed interested in other Goju stylists. He knew of my previous club and had met my former instructor Chris Rowen. He explained his club always trained on mats, so they could work on throws and grappling. They considered ground fighting a vital element of their training. He assured me these techniques were an integral part of Goju Ryu karate.

Soon the room began to fill up. I was surprised to see the sheer size of the class. There were well over thirty people, bouncing around, chatting and stretching. They all seemed very fit and raring to go. At eight o'clock Sensei Gavin called the class to order. I found myself at the head of a long line that snaked all the way to the back of the hall. He began with a traditional bow, though less formal than I was used to. After a brief warm-up and stretch, he had the class doing press-ups, sit-ups and squats. My fitness was not what it used to be, and I struggled to keep up.

When he called for light sparring, I turned and bowed to the guy next to me. I began to spar in my usual way, light and fast, attacking to the face, neck and groin. I assumed all Goju clubs sparred this way. I was in for a shock. My opponent walked straight through these strikes and hit me with a hard combination to the body, then dropped a low kick onto my thigh. I felt echoes of long ago.

Gavin shouted 'Go to ground!' and suddenly we were wrestling on the floor. I had some experience from my days in judo, but my lack of fitness meant I was quickly overpowered. After a few more rounds of sparring and grappling, I was exhausted. These guys were seriously fit and very up for it.

There were a lot of girls in the club and their attitude impressed me. They were very determined and didn't hesitate to get stuck in. The next highest grade to me was a tall, slim girl with long dark hair. Now we faced each other to spar.

I'd found the other black belts tough and strong, but their attacks were relatively simple. She was different. She launched some fast strikes to my head, and then switched easily to the body. As I covered up she caught me with a low kick and another face punch. She seemed able to switch at will. She also had great control. This was exciting.

I relaxed a little and began throwing a few lighter, faster combinations. She countered perfectly and sped up again. Soon we were fighting, fast and flowing. Once in a while, one of us would land a strike through the defences. The other would acknowledge with the faintest nod and that great universal dojo word: 'Oooouss'.

When Sensei told us to go to the ground, she wrapped her legs around my torso and put her hands inside my lapels. Before I knew it, she'd dragged me in close and had me in a vicious strangle.

We changed partners and she went off to torment someone else. I turned to face another girl. She was small, and looked lovely and gentle. She was only a brown belt. I decided to go easy on her, not because I was a gentleman, I was just knackered. I pushed her onto her back and she wrapped her legs around me, just like the previous girl. (This position is the 'guard' and if you're on the floor and *underneath*, it's a good position to be in.)

I wasn't worried. I was on top. I could have a breather. I reached forward in a light hearted attempt at a strangle. Next thing I knew, her leg had swung across my face and my arm was in a powerful lock. Using all my strength against this small girl, I prised it free. I was relieved I hadn't tapped out (submitted). Before I knew what was happening, she'd flipped me onto my back. She'd got my lapel and somehow wrapped it around my neck. Now she was hanging onto it with her entire bodyweight and strangling the living daylights out of me. I felt the blood rush to my head. I remember thinking I really didn't want to submit. Then I blacked out.

I came to a moment later. Thankfully, she'd eased the pressure, thinking her strangle wasn't working. As the lights came back on in my head, I felt her flip across my back and sure enough, a new strangle came on from the other side. I had no idea where she was. I got my hands to my neck just in time to stop her. I moved into her, pushing her onto her back. She seemed completely at ease there. As soon as I moved my arm, she had it in another lock.

Sensei Gavin called a halt to the grappling and I was spared further embarrassment. The class gathered round and he began teaching a variety of self-defence techniques. We practised with partners. He would occasionally show me where the technique came from in the kata. It seemed he could go on all night with different strikes, locks, throws, strangles. He was clearly a vast source of knowledge and knew countless kata applications that I'd never seen before.

By the end of the lesson, I'd made up my mind. The man had a great deal to teach me. He could take me down new avenues that I'd not explored before. I signed up there and then.

A core of students retired to the local pub for beers or soft drinks. I was invited to join them. There was an enjoyable atmosphere. Gavin held court, laughing and joking and regaling us with tales of working on the door and travelling around Japan and China. He'd trained with some of the top Goju masters in the UK and abroad.

I was soon a regular at the club. For the first few weeks, my lack of fitness made me easy prey for some of the stronger fighters, and I needed all my skill to defend myself. Still, I wasn't too worried. I knew it was only a matter of time before my fitness returned. It would come back naturally to meet the rigours of this new, more physical training regime. And in my spare time I began running and pushing weights, just to get my strength up.

As my fitness returned, so did my confidence. My old full-contact style was beginning to come back to me, and I wasn't getting the same stick any more. Better still, I felt myself moving more naturally than ever before. I began to think no one at the club could really trouble me.

Then a black belt turned up who I'd not met before. He was obviously well-known there. His name was Mark. He looked big and powerful. He chatted amicably to some of the others. But when it was time to spar, he was quite serious. I threw a couple of light, friendly kicks to set the tone, but he wasn't having any of it. Suddenly, a front kick lashed out from nowhere and caught me in the stomach. I stumbled back across the room.

Mark was a serious fighter. I stepped up the pace, but he was simply too good. I couldn't get through. He was that nasty combination of being strong *and* fast. Worse still, his timing was excellent, and he was deadly accurate. He was as good a fighter as I had ever come across, and equally at home on the ground. I needed to get a lot stronger and fitter before I could stand up to him.

Mark seemed to be the strongest fighter in the club. But there was another guy, more senior than Mark, who I still hadn't met. I'd only heard his name spoken in awed tones. It was Carl. People went on about his power, his skill, his timing, his kicks. He sounded unbeatable. He played with people at tournaments. Toyed with them. He could kick you to the head three times before you knew what was happening. Soon I was sick and tired of hearing about this Carl. I was keen to see what all the fuss was about.

Even Gavin spoke highly his ability in sparring. I wanted to see what he could do for myself. I'd seen some great fighters in my time and didn't believe anyone could be quite as good as they were making out. It was only when I heard that Carl was an ex Kyokushinkai champion that the penny finally dropped. 'I know him,' I shouted. 'He's from my old club!'

When I finally met Carl, he'd hardly changed. Just a few grey hairs had crept in. He took a moment to place me because I'd been a lowly green belt when we last trained together. 'Didn't you fight lightweight?' he asked, noticing my extra girth.

'Yeah, I'm definitely middleweight now,' I laughed.

It was good to catch up and talk about the old days. But Carl only put in rare appearances. He was living far outside London.

After a while, I got used to standing at the head of the class. People began to refer to me as Sempai, the class senior. I felt deeply honoured by this title, and very unworthy. In my mind, a Sempai was someone far above me. Someone like my first Sempai, Gary Malcolm, at the club in Tottenham where Carl and I had first met.

But later, on reflection, I realised that apart from Gavin himself, there was no one in the club who knew more about karate than me. I enjoyed helping people out with advice and guidance. Maybe I could get used to the role of Sempai after all. I decided to try to follow the example of my first Sempai. I could think of none better.

And strangely, just around that time, I bumped into Gary Malcolm in the street. Perhaps it was my old friend the Tao at work again, because it was a very timely twist of fate. I remember most vividly…

I was walking out of an advertising agency on Wardour Street when I noticed a tall motorcycle messenger in black leathers and helmet coming in. Just as he was striding to the door, a woman walked right in front of him, oblivious that he was even there. He pulled up suddenly, to avoid bumping into her, and she walked on, still unaware. Something about the motorcyclist's courtesy and awareness impressed me, and I held the door open for him to come in.

We passed in the doorway and I went out across the road. Then I hear someone calling me. It was the motorcyclist. He'd come back outside and was taking off his helmet. It was Gary Malcolm. I hadn't seen him in years, but he looked exactly the same. He'd recognised me.

We chatted for a while and caught up about karate. He was now the Sensei at the Tottenham club. He was interested to hear what I was doing. I told him about my training and promised to come by and visit some time. Then we shook hands warmly and parted ways.

I was buzzing all afternoon after that meeting. If you don't do martial arts, it may be hard for you to understand the importance we place in the people that teach us. They are not like schoolteachers or lecturers, where the tuition is compulsory. In martial arts the teaching and the learning is all voluntary. It's a shared passion. The rewards of your instructor's lessons go deep.

So I was dismayed to hear, not long after that meeting, that Gary died, tragically young, from a serious illness. At the

28th National Knockdown Tournament in 2003 they held a minute's silence in his honour. I was in the audience and the silence touched me deeply. I reflected how Gary had helped me go from a green beginner to a reasonable fighter, and set me firmly on the path I was following now. His passing was a sad loss to the martial arts.

Being the club Sempai wasn't entirely ceremonial. With it went the dubious honour of being Sensei's *Uke*. This is the person he demonstrates on. The fall guy. For years I'd watched my Senseis performing on hapless Ukes, whose attacks would be effortlessly deflected before getting a right old pasting. I'd wince as they got kicked, punched, locked, choked, gouged, strangled and picked up by their skin … and thank my lucky stars it wasn't me out there.

Now it was. But I was quite proud to be Gavin's Uke. It *was* an honour. It was my time. Now it was me getting the treatment, to the accompaniment of sharp intakes of breath from the audience. After each demo Gavin would ask 'Does anyone need to see that again?' with a wicked grin on his face. Some bugger would always say yes.

Gavin had years of experience in security work and often lectured on Control and Restraint to doormen. He must have known a hundred ways of marching someone out of a room in varying degrees of agony. I felt each one, several times.

Soon he began asking me to take a warm-up, or instruct the lower belts at the back of the class. Then he asked me to take a couple of lessons while he was away. I was very nervous and planned my first lesson carefully in advance. I even made a crib sheet and left it on the table at the front of the dojo.

At eight o'clock sharp I called the class to order with a shout. No one responded. There were too many people banging away at pads and bags. I took a deep breath and bellowed out the command to line up again. This time they responded. I took the class through my usual warm-up and moved straight into my carefully planned syllabus. It went like clockwork and I completed everything I'd set out to do. I was delighted. Then I checked the clock and realised it was only eight-thirty. I still had an hour to fill.

The second time I took a class, I slowed everything to a more natural pace and it worked better. But towards the end, I wanted to try some high level teaching with the brown and black belts. I split the class up and went through some advanced concepts with them. I tried to impart all the things I'd learned about the development of natural momentum and the flow of chi. I was met with a sea of blank faces. I soon sensed they were getting frustrated. It wasn't working. I switched back to more basic exercises until the end of the class.

The third time I took a lesson, I abandoned all my carefully planned formulas and gave them the workout from hell. They did press-ups, sit-ups, squats and pad work until their knuckles were raw and their mouths were hanging open. To my surprise, they loved it. Several women ran up to me afterwards to tell me how much they'd enjoyed themselves. Even Gavin heard favourable reports and rang to tell me.

Through teaching, I'd learned a valuable lesson myself. You can't rush your progress in karate. A beginner shouldn't be working on the same things as a black belt. Each stage needs to be understood, assimilated and savoured before moving onto the next. A fighter needs to build firm foundations before going higher.

The simple, hard physical training I'd done early on was what I'd needed at the time. It had developed my fitness, power, determination and spirit. The bedrock for any fighter. Skill and technique are important too, but they take far longer to acquire and you still need fitness and determination to make them work.

Shihan, Hanshi

People are always fascinated by the grading system in karate. What's the highest belt? Who is the highest grade in the world? How can I become a tenth dan?

Over the years I've been fortunate enough to train with several masters of karate and other systems. The answer to these questions about the highest levels is that it is less about what you do and more about what you *know*. These masters have a lifetime of experience to share. Like the great boxing trainers, they understand how a fighting system works and how to train young people to achieve their maximum potential.

In my system of karate, the last grading is fifth dan. For this level, the instructor is assessed on their ability to teach black belts and junior instructors. The title awarded after the fifth dan has been achieved is Shihan (master) – teacher of teachers. Further dan grades are then awarded according to years of service and the ability to grow and develop an organisation.

I was delighted to be at both Sensei Gavin's and Sensei Dan's fifth dan grading. They each took a basic kata and spent several hours taking it apart, showing how the principles contained in the movements could lead to almost infinite self-defence applications. It was an inspiring experience.

So when Gavin announced that his own instructor would be holding a seminar, I was intrigued. The guy was an eighth dan, one of the highest grades in the country. His title was *Kyoshi*, which means 'mentor'. Gavin held him in the highest regard, which was unusual and meant a lot. I was excited to see the man in person and a little nervous. I'd probably be his Uke for the demonstrations. I wondered what was in store.

The seminar was on *Okinawan Te* (Okinawan hand); the precursor to Kara Te, now written as karate (empty hand). It was restricted to higher grades so we could cover some more advanced techniques.

When he arrived outside the dojo in his civilian clothes, Gavin's instructor seemed unremarkable. Medium height, close cropped greying hair, taciturn. But once in his gi, he seemed to come alive. The room was filled with row upon row of brown and black belts. As he began teaching, he moved with effortless power and grace. He showed basic footwork patterns and made it look very easy, but when I tried it, I couldn't move the same way. Then he asked for a volunteer so he could demonstrate a technique. I stepped forward but Gavin got there first.

It was interesting to see our instructor on the receiving end, for a change. Even the man in charge had a man in charge of him. Pretty soon Gavin was being smashed and thrown around the room in fine style. His humility was admirable. But after a while, his teacher decided it was a bit much to keep using our Sensei and called for another volunteer. This was my cue.

Standing near him I felt an ominous power bristling in front of me. His hands and arms seemed to be made of hard wood. Rather than blocking my attacks he would deflect and trap my arm at the wrist, often striking at the same time. I felt my arm in a vice-like grip. With a simple shift in his body weight or position, a painful lock would go on. I'd be forced to roll or have my joint broken. By altering his position again I'd be sent sprawling across the room.

As he demonstrated he talked of principles, a common theme in karate. Principles hold true whatever the situation. Then towards the end of the session, he moved onto pressure points. These are sensitive areas around the body and some martial arts study them in depth. He asked me to take off my top, so he could show the points more easily. I complied nervously. I'd heard he could break wood with his fingers. Having felt the strength in his hands, I had no doubt it was true.

A strike to a pressure point could easily knock me out or make me ill, if it was hard enough. As he walked around me, talking of points and meridians, I expected a sharp blow at any moment. I felt like a swimmer being circled by a shark. But while he prodded and poked his hard fingers into my neck, head, body and arms, nothing worse than that was done.

To end the session, he explained how a basic knowledge of healing should go hand in hand with fighting. He laid me down on the floor and, taking me by the ankles, swung my legs left and right before laying them down flat. He checked my pelvic alignment and asked if I had pain in my lower back on the left side? I have always suffered in exactly that spot. He pushed hard against one of my thighs and then, turning me onto my side, stretched my lower back like an expert physiotherapist.

Turning me on my front, he worked up the back, pushing his dangerous fingers into the points along my spine in the style of a shiatsu massage, explaining as he went along. When I got to my feet, I felt good. My back is almost always stiff, but now it felt loose and relaxed.

Things began to make sense. The 'points' on the body have been known for thousands of years through traditional Chinese medicine. Massaged therapeutically, they can be used to improve health and well-being. Struck hard, they could injure or kill. It was simply a question of degree.

He explained that in Okinawa, before the advent of 'sport' karate, practitioners would train hard and then help each other relieve tired muscles to reduce soreness the next day. Not for the first time, I was struck with the similarities to Western boxing. Trainers often massage fighters after a hard workout to help muscles recover more quickly.

There is a lot of therapeutic practice in karate, though it's not immediately obvious. The classic Goju stance of *Sanchin* (which is also a kata in its own right) helps to develop a more correct posture, strengthening the lower abdominal muscles that support the spine and improving pelvic alignment. Again, there was no real mystery here. It was all just common sense.

This fascinating session showed how training in martial arts can go in a circular path, from learning to injure, to learning to heal.

Some months later, our club was invited to take part in an Aikido demonstration. The head of a famous Japanese association, a ninth dan, was visiting the UK, and the demo was being held in his honour. We watched some excellent displays of fast, flowing Aikido from the UK and then, to change the mood a little, a bunch from our club did some kata, self-defence and breaking.

Ten of us stood in a row with a partner holding a one-inch wooden board. Starting at one end, we went along and broke the boards one after the other, vying to make the most impressive break. Some of the girls broke with a punch, which is always a crowd-pleaser. Mark smashed his board with his head. I decided to use the back of my wrist. I'd tried it a couple of times in class, with mixed success. This time, with hundreds of people watching, I was determined not to bounce off the bloody thing. I smashed through it and almost hit Brian, who was holding it.

Sensei Gavin then dropped his board with one hand and punched it in half with the other as it fell. It's a very difficult break, because there's no resistance. The punch has to be very fast and accurate.

The visiting grandmaster seemed pleased by our demonstration. There was a party on a boat on the Thames afterwards. What struck me was how he was treated with such great respect by his association. He'd come with his own translator from Japan, an Aikido black belt himself, who attended to his every need and even helped the old man take off his shoes at the edge of the mat. The old gentleman was being honoured and revered by his association for the lifetime of teaching and service he'd put in.

Later that same year, we had a seminar by a tenth dan grandmaster who'd come all the way from Okinawa. The head of an association is normally given the honorary title of Hanshi (or Kancho or Sosei) though this master, like many, was happy to be addressed as Sensei. To be someone's Sensei is always considered a great honour.

As Gavin's 'cultural ambassador', I was asked to collect the visiting grandmaster from Heathrow and take him to his London hotel. I was fascinated to meet a real-life tenth dan in person. He'd come to the UK with his representative from Canada, a seventh dan, but spoke reasonable English himself.

When I heard they had a day to kill in London before the seminar, I jumped at the chance to show them around. We met the next morning and walked around London's main sights. For once, the weather didn't let us down. Big Ben, the Houses of Parliament and Buckingham Palace all looked resplendent in the sunshine. Then we hailed a traditional London cab and drove past Hyde Park to Regent Street, where we stopped in ye olde Starbucks for a Frappuccino.

The grandmaster was 60 but in excellent shape. He was a quiet and composed man, not in the least conceited by his rank and an easy companion. Better still, he seemed delighted with my impromptu tour. I was pleased he got to see London at its best.

In the evening we made our way to the dojo for the seminar. He taught us a new kata that his father had added to their family syllabus and we did our best to follow. He showed some applications and his associate performed an outstanding version of the well-known kata Sanseryu. He was incredibly calm and peaceful man, but at the end of the seminar he invited Carl to punch and kick him as hard as he could. Carl threw several of his 'big whammies' into the man with no effect. He was as solid as a rock and attributed it to practising the kata *Sanchin* with his father since the age of five.

Shortly after he returned to Okinawa, I received an email. He thanked me for showing him around London and told me I had an open invitation to visit his dojo. I was honoured that he'd taken the trouble, me being a lowly third dan and all. He was a gentleman and one day, I hope to take him up on his invitation.

I realised the higher levels of martial arts are not so different from any other organisation. Like an army or a corporation, the leaders have done their time in the trenches. Now they are prized for their ability to plan, organise and inspire the rest of the group. The highest grades are awards for a lifetime of devotion to disseminating the martial arts so new people can follow the same path.

Sadly, the grading system has been badly abused in recent years. You can order a black belt complete with genuine certificate off the internet, Britain is full to bursting with self-appointed tenth dans and of course in America there are ninjas as high as fifteenth dan. Scary stuff.

Testing Grounds

When our club had a grading, I went along to help out. It was for novices and lower belts so I was expecting a low-key affair. Some chance. When it started, I was shocked by the level of intensity that Sensei Gavin was demanding. After a punishing warm-up and fitness test the students were drilled relentlessly in basics, kata and bunkai. Then after a hard pad session, they began sparring. The thuds of hard punches and kicks brought back memories of serious knockdown training.

When everyone was well and truly knackered, Gavin called me out with Mark and Moz, a giant brown belt who was an experienced doorman. Each student had to fight us in turn. First me, then Moz, then Mark. They were very tired but some of them were big guys and very pumped up. I had to hit them with everything I had to avoid being overpowered. Once I'd finished with them, I passed them along to grapple with Moz and then Mark put on the finishing touches. I was knackered by the end.

A few months later, Gavin announced the annual tournament. It was a relatively low-key affair between our club and a sister club in Bristol, run by Sensei Dan Lewis. There were perhaps sixty or seventy entrants. The categories were points sparring, grappling and kata. Gavin told me that as a third dan, I was not obliged to compete. I said I would anyway. I needed the incentive to get into better shape. And I was also interested to see how my new knowledge would serve me. Could I control my nerves any better now?

I found that I could. I still felt some nerves, of course. But using what I'd learned from my research, I managed to keep my mind positive. I trained purposefully to win. I pictured myself against the most difficult opponents and visualised scoring points, over and over again. I worked on some of the touch-fighting drills I'd picked up over the years. And I sang a little ditty over and over to myself, like a mantra. It made me smile and kept my mind positive.

On the day of the tournament, we made our way to Bristol in a convoy of cars. Halfway along the M4 we stopped off for breakfast at a service station. This time, instead of being wrapped up in my own mental turmoil, I looked for it in the others instead. As we sat in the cafeteria, some were tapping their feet nervously, others were laughing a little too loud or sitting in a silent world of their own. Everyone was nervous, although some were acting as if they weren't. After eating a big breakfast at least one person puked it up again. Everyone visited the toilet before rejoining the convoy.

These were all the effects of nerves and perfectly normal. I was noticing them in others for the first time. The signs continued at the tournament. People began to make excuses. They had an injury. They had a cold. They weren't sure if they could fight. They moaned if they got a bad pairing in the opening round.

I took some satisfaction from seeing all this. They were showing weakness, lack of resolve. I drew strength from it. I felt my confidence grow. I was already fully committed to fighting the best person at the tournament. I wasn't bothered when that would be. First, last or any time was fine by me. I'd already accepted the idea and trained with that in mind. Let's get it on.

In my head, I'd fought and beaten Mark many times. But whether I could do it for real was another matter. If I felt a rush of nerves, I hummed my little ditty to myself, over and over, and it made me feel good again. *'Ooh, stick you, your mama too, and your daddy'*, a great little tune by Daphne and Celeste. Try singing it to yourself if you get nervous. You'll find you really can't feel worried any more.

I could see people from Bristol eyeing me nervously, wondering how good I was. I put on my best relaxed air, warming up nonchalantly and throwing a few techniques, not enough to give away too much of my style.

My first fight was against a young purple belt guy from Bristol. He must have been the same level as I'd been in my very first tournament. Now the shoe was on the other foot. I was the third dan. He was the coloured belt. He looked fit and determined, just as I had been. Would I have the skill to beat him?

Sure enough, he came charging into me from the opening bell. I saw a high kick coming, but he was a little too far away. I knew it wouldn't connect. As it rose I brushed it past my face. I knew he'd land with his back to me, so I moved in and caught him with a punch in the side, shouting a loud '*kiai*'. I scored half a point instantly. One more and I'd win.

I suspected that losing a half a point so quickly would drive him to try even harder. I was right. But this time, when he rushed in, he stuck to punches, which were harder for me to score against. I parried and hit back. We cancelled each other out. No one scored a clean strike.

The referee broke us up and we returned to our starting lines. I could see he was still very up for it, bristling and ready to go. He was showing good spirit, but by now, I knew what he was going to do. He was going to rush in again.

I had an idea, but it was high risk. If I could stop his rush with a spinning back kick, I would win the fight. But if I missed, I would expose my back and he could score easily. As he came rushing in again, I was still in two minds. I stepped back, one, two paces, to avoid the punches. I was at the edge of the mat, cornered and the momentum was his. I was in danger of losing a point anyway. It was now or never…

I jumped and spun, saying a prayer (a very short one) and lashed out with my back leg. The sole of my foot felt a reassuring thud. It landed squarely in his stomach and the referee stopped the match. I'd won.

My next fight was against a different fighter all together. It was Mark. As we squared up, I sang my little ditty and imagined myself scoring against him, just as I had in my training. The referee called us to our starting lines and shouted '*Hajime!*' (begin). Mark stood poised and ready. I edged closer. He stayed still. This type of fighting is sudden-death. The first person to score one full point or two half points is the winner. I decided to strike first.

I lunged forward, swept his guard aside with my left and landed a big right hand into his body. He reacted with a counter, but it was a little late. I scored a half point. My plan was working perfectly. All my visualisation was coming true. I needed just one more strike to win. It seemed almost too easy.

It was. Mark is one of those fighters who needs a reason to be at his best. I had just given him one. He unleashed a barrage of punches and kicks that was unstoppable. I stepped back and veered to the side to evade the onslaught. He stayed on top of me, driving me right off the mat. I blocked several punches and kicks, but others got through. I had no answer. He scored a half point and we were even.

Now we eyed each other cautiously. The next point would be the winner. Neither wanted to make a foolish mistake. Mark was poised to attack. So was I. We had both shown our cards, I had to strike soon, before he launched another barrage, but my confidence was a bit shaken. I had to stay positive and keep my mind right. I moved around, out of his range, and pictured myself catching him again with fast footwork and a sudden blitz attack. And to fool him, I would switch to south paw (right foot forward) just before I struck.

I bounced slightly to keep him guessing. He stood poised. Coming closer, I switched my stance quickly to disguise the strike and lunged forward. A perfect front kick sailed straight into my gut. It was a clear point. An instant win.

Dammit. I'd been messing around with fancy footwork and got caught by a simple front kick. I was angry with myself. Why was I fooling about instead of keeping it simple? This was no time to experiment against such a good opponent. When we stepped off the mat, the timekeeper told us the entire fight had lasted just 17 seconds.

In the end I went home with just a Silver medal for kata. I'd lost in the final to one of the girls. Oh well, she had performed her kata very well. In general, the women did kata better than the guys. Instead of using muscular power and aggression, they used natural body movements. Their technique was more correct. They had natural grace, which kata tries to teach us. With grace comes efficiency and hence effectiveness.

I was glad I'd gone along and it was good to meet the instructor from Bristol, Dan Lewis, who was the joint chief instructor of my new association.

The next time I saw him was at summer camp. The association met up for three days at a scouts camp in Portishead near Bristol. There were three sessions per day plus early morning fitness for people who were grading. I was asked to take these sessions, which involved an early rise and 30 minutes of sprints and conditioning exercises. Then we'd wolf down a quick breakfast before the day's training began in earnest. We covered everything from kata and bunkai to fitness work, pad work and (a new area for me) weapons.

Gavin and Dan managed to make all the hard work most enjoyable. Their humour helped to keep spirits up when they began to flag. They displayed new depths that I'd not seen before. When it came to weapons, Gavin took a two hour session with the four foot staff or *Jo*. I'd had no idea he was so good with a stick.

Next, Dan taught how to use *Escrima* sticks. These are two light rattan sticks wielded together. He began with simple drills which I did my best to follow. In between, he would show more advanced sequences and the sticks would blur around him, describing perfect circles and arcs, cutting the air with sharp whooshes. His skill was astonishing.

Not to be outdone, Gavin took a two hour course on knives. One of the black belts held a training knife to Gavin's stomach and he clapped his hands expertly around the wrist. The knife flew off into the audience. It wasn't as easy as it looked when I tried myself. We practised various disarms against a knife attacker. It's one of the most difficult and dangerous self-defence scenarios you can imagine.

Gavin moved onto knife fighting, where both combatants have a blade. He called me out to attack him. I had never done it before and had no idea what to expect. I lunged forward to stab him in the belly. He parried my arm at the wrist, sliced across my forearm and continued slicing up my arm before stabbing into my collarbone and across my windpipe. I'd been carved up like a spit roast and for the next hour, he continued to demonstrate his culinary expertise.

Gavin had asked me to prepare a ten-minute talk as part of my own incorporation into the association. I decided to cover the much misunderstood topic of *ju* or 'softness'. That evening by the campfire I droned on for an hour about the importance of relaxation as well as tension. Some seemed to grasp what I was saying, while others couldn't comprehend that softness could be as dangerous as hardness. There were some questions afterwards which I answered as fully as I could.

On the second day, Carl completed his Thirty Man Kumite. He fought his way through 30 of the highest grades in the association and set the mood of the camp alight with his achievement. A new level of testing had been set and it sent an ominous message to the black belts. They realised what awaited them if they ever wanted to reach second dan. I was relieved that I wouldn't have to do it myself, being a third dan already.

On the last day, I joined in with some parts of the black belt grading along with a newcomer to the club, Steve. He was a black belt who'd been training in Japan and had stopped off in London on his way home to Canada. He enjoyed training with us so much, he ended up staying several years.

At the end of summer camp, Steve and I were awarded a club badge to sew onto our gi. This little piece of cloth carried a lot of meaning. It showed Gavin and Dan were happy for us to represent their association at our current grades anywhere in the world. I was deeply honoured. I'm sure Steve was too.

Ups and Downs

Around this time, life took a new turn. My wife and I had grown distant over the last few years. Our children seemed to be the only thing we shared a delight in. It's difficult to say exactly why a couple grow apart and the excuses all sound like clichés: we met very young; we grew into different people; we wanted different things out of life. Maybe we just stopped trying.

I don't blame karate, because there were many more factors involved. But if I'd directed the same energy into my marriage, perhaps things would have turned out differently. After many weeks of agonising, we agreed to get a divorce.

Telling the children was easily the worst day of my life. I moved out shortly afterwards. The split was what they call 'amicable' and I had unlimited access to the kids. I stayed very close to them and they stayed with me every weekend. Nevertheless, the split hit me hard, and I found myself in a deep depression.

I continued training. Hitting the heavy bag was quite therapeutic, but I was far from my best. I began to understand why master

Miyagi advised his students to attend to family first, work second and karate third. If you're unhappy in your home life and relationships or worried about work, you can't settle down and concentrate on your training. You need to feel secure, deep down, before you can apply yourself fully.

I took comfort from the knowledge that things could only get better. Life would soon get more exciting. I was young, free and single. All right, I was 35, free and single. But the world was my oyster. I could do as I pleased. Yet leaving my children made me feel so guilty, I could think of little else.

At work, my colleagues could see I was in a bad way. One friend recommended seeing a counsellor. He told me it had helped him through a difficult time. He was one of the last people I'd have expected to suggest something so touchy-feely, so I decided to give it a try.

I visited a lady in Walthamstow and ended up going back once a week for several months. It was very helpful, like speaking to your favourite aunt, without worrying that she's part of the family. I could say anything I wanted and there was no come-back. The simple act of verbalising frustrations is a great way to get rid of them.

She wasn't interested in my wife, my children, my parents, my sister or my friends. She was only interested in me. It felt naughty but nice, to talk about myself. We'd make lists of what I wanted. Only me. Now I'm sure I'm as selfish as the next man, but I'd always been brought up to put others first, at least on paper. It felt strange and wonderful to sit with her, planning all sorts of self-indulgent things for myself.

I was busy planning exotic holidays when the annual karate tournament came around. I decided to give it a miss. As the club's Sempai, I was expected to perform to a certain standard at all times. Sure, I wasn't expected to win everything, but it wouldn't look good if I was beaten too easily. I spoke to Gavin and told him I'd be staying away. He understood and reminded me that the tournament was not compulsory for me anyway.

That year, due to growing numbers, a new black belt section was created. Steve waltzed through it, winning gold in sparring, grappling and kata. I was not surprised. He was very good and in excellent shape.

Meanwhile I'd started going out on dates. I didn't seem to have any trouble meeting beautiful women. There were plenty in the smart ad agencies of central London. But once we got past the pleasantries and talked more seriously, things would go awry. A newly divorced man is not exactly a barrel of laughs and I must have been miserable company. I stopped dating for a while until I got over my depression.

At the club's annual summer camp, Mark and Charlie successfully completed their Thirty Man Kumite. By that time I felt stronger, and enjoyed taking part in Mark's line-up and giving him a bit of stick in his last fight.

By the end of the summer, I began to feel good again. My children had grown accustomed to the split. I still saw them every weekend and we all got used to the new arrangements.

I became friendly with one of the girls from the club, Charmaigne. We would chat in the pub after training, or pop to McDonalds for a bite to eat. Soon, we began dating, all very formally and correctly, since she was Charlie's twin sister and that made her Gavin's sister-in-law.

As we got more serious, I wondered if it was wise to mix karate and relationships? I'd always used training as a refuge from the pressures of work and home. Now the boundaries had blurred. But I realised there with some cool benefits, too. When I told Charmaigne I wanted to train at the weekend, she would say she wished she was as dedicated as me. It sounded so strange, I wondered if she was being sarcastic. She wasn't.

We moved in together and life began to look up. I went on trip to Kerala in South India, which I'd been planning all year. It felt good travelling alone, doing exactly as I pleased. I didn't feel guilty for leaving Charmaigne, because by coincidence, she'd planned a trip to the Caribbean at the same time. She went with her mother and sister to Dominica, where her family came from. When we got back together we had lots of adventures to talk about.

Soon the tournament came around again. I was back to my usual form so I decided to enter. There was an added bonus too. Steve had gone back to Canada and neither Mark nor Carl could make it. I was the most senior black belt and favourite to win the black belt section. The pressure was quite intense, but I was determined not to let it ruin my chances.

I devised a training routine to get into shape, with plenty of sprints and footwork drills. I worked on developing explosive speed and power. To get my head together, I visualised scoring points, over and over again. I hummed my favourite little song and imagined my opponents floundering under my attacks. This time felt better. I'd been training with Gavin for several years and I felt much stronger, fully fit and ready to go.

Charmaigne and I drove to Bristol and stayed overnight in a hotel. It meant a relaxing morning, instead of getting up at the crack of dawn and sitting in traffic on the M4. When I got to the tournament, I was feeling relaxed and confident. There were eight black belts in my section. They were all good fighters, and I knew I'd have to be on top form to win. I hummed to myself and threw a few relaxed combinations to keep moving.

After a couple of hours of waiting, the fighting began. I was up against experienced fighters. One mistake and I'd lose. I played very safe. When I attacked, it was with full commitment. The rest of the time, I stayed alert and ready, just waiting for my opponent to make a mistake. There was no in-between. No tricksy footwork. I was taking no chances. As soon as I saw the slightest opening, I took it. My reverse punch was landing nicely. I grew in confidence. When my opponents attacked, I seemed to know what they were doing. I evaded everything. The moment their momentum waned, I fired right back and scored.

To my delight, I won all my fights in short order and took the gold medal. I don't think anyone scored even a half point against me. That day, I was flying. I was very pleased with myself. It was my best performance ever. To top it all, I won gold in the grappling too, beating an experienced jujitsu fighter. It was an unexpected bonus.

The only thing left to win was the kata. This was where I felt most confident. The countless hours I'd spent on kata meant I could always put in a strong performance. I coasted through the early rounds with my most spectacular kata, Seipai. It's a beautiful flowing kata that's only taught to higher grades. I knew it was a crowd-pleaser and milked it for all it was worth.

In the final, I found myself competing head-to-head with Charlie, who was heavily pregnant at the time. We were asked to perform another advanced kata, *Shisochin*, side by side. When we finished, I was very pleased with my performance. I was convinced I'd won. The corner judges were asked for a decision and I expected to see four flags pointing in my direction. To my surprise, two of them pointed towards Charlie.

She was talented at kata, but surely mine had been better? Now it was up to Gavin and Dan to decide. I was certain they'd appreciate the genius of my work. Gavin leaned across to Dan and they murmured to each other. Then, to my horror, they awarded the gold to Charlie. She squealed with delight and hugged me. I did my best to be a good loser, but I still haven't forgiven her. She cheated by having a lower centre of gravity.

That aside, it had been a very good day and boosted my confidence immeasurably. My karate had reached a new height and it spurred me on to train even more seriously. There was still a lot to look forward to that year. At summer camp, it would be Steve's turn to attempt the Thirty Man Kumite along with Jay, one of our female black belts.

Steve had been away for a year, training in Toronto, and saving up for a flight to the UK. He was coming back with the sole purpose of doing the Thirty Man Kumite. I could think of better ways to spend my holidays, but Steve was that kind of guy.

As I prepared for summer camp with fitness work and weapons drills, I wondered about the Thirty Man Kumite myself. I didn't have to do it. I was already a third dan and my grade was fully recognised. But if I requested it, I knew Gavin and Dan would arrange it for me. They loved watching people get stuck in.

Each time I considered it, worrying images pushed their way into my mind. Great fighters like Carl and Mark had been at the edge of exhaustion, barely able to defend themselves. I told myself to be sensible. I didn't need it. I had other things to think about: teaching, weapons, grappling.... I was the Sempai. I needed to keep my dignity. What if I failed? Life at the club would be unbearable.

I decided to leave it to Steve and his contemporaries to worry about and put all thoughts of the Thirty Man Kumite aside.

Dark Clouds

The blue skies have deserted us this year. Grey clouds have been hanging over us since the start of summer camp and there have been several downpours. By the afternoon of the second day, the rain has turned into a drizzle, and then a refreshing spray so fine, it's little more than a vapour.

We're back on the Field of Truth and Steve is preparing for his Thirty Man Kumite. He's wearing a light waterproof jacket over his gi and pacing up and down, staring into the middle distance and mouthing silent words to himself. Occasionally he pummels himself lightly in the belly, to ready himself for what's ahead.

He moves carefully from one foot to another. I notice he avoids bouncing, and with good reason. One of his feet is broken. Earlier in the week, he'd had one last, hard sparring session in the dojo and injured his foot. A small bone was broken and he's been hobbling all week.

There's no question of Steve cancelling his test. Not because Sensei is cruel or unsympathetic. Simply because Steve has flown all the way from Canada to do it. Achieving his second dan grade under Gavin and

Dan means that much to him. Gavin reassured Steve that if he failed his test, it wouldn't be because of his foot. He's full of reassuring tips like that.

I know Steve has trained incredibly hard for his test. He's a tough and able fighter, and though he's less experienced than Mark or Carl, I know he'll make up for it in fitness and determination.

Steve has been unable to find a karate club in Toronto to his liking, so he's trained in Thai Boxing, and Systema, a martial art devised by Russian Special Forces. He has adopted a Spartan lifestyle, following punishing fitness routines at ungodly hours and forsaking a normal social life. He has even taken work as a doorman to develop his self-belief and confidence. A big part of getting through a test like the Thirty Man Kumite is believing, deep down, that you've earned the right to pass. If you have any doubts, they will quickly grow into acceptance of defeat when things get nasty.

Steve is tall, well over six feet, and normally weighs over 13 stone. But he's come back lighter than usual. His plan was to keep moving, rather than stand and slug. It was a good plan, until his accident. Now he's going to have a problem. When he'd joined in my morning fitness session, he could barely walk.

But that doesn't matter now. Now the adrenaline is kicking in. It will mask the pain for a while. That's what Gavin had meant when he'd said the injury wouldn't prevent Steve from passing.

Steve is not the only one taking his test today. Jay is attempting it too. She is standing stoically beside Steve as a long line of women forms up. It doesn't look like there are enough to make 30 people, so she will have to fight some women twice. Or knowing our instructors, they will send a few guys over to keep Jay on her toes.

She's in remarkably good spirits. She has been all week. Jay is in her element and loves getting stuck in, testing her spirit. This is her big chance. It looks like it could be the happiest day of her life. I wish I could be so chirpy before a big test.

Steve's line-up is ready now. As usual, there's little ceremony. He bows to 30 people. As the first fighter steps forward, the rain stops right on cue. The cool weather is a good thing. The only worry is the slippery grass.

Steve's first fight is Yoshi, an experienced Kyokushin fighter from Japan. Though small and slight, he's very powerful, with devastating high kicks. He's never hurt anyone with them, but there's always a sense that he's holding back. He has never met Steve before, and it makes a fascinating opening bout.

They fight with determination and intensity, exchanging hard punches and kicks, neither giving ground. At one point Steve catches Yoshi with a big front kick and knocks him back several feet. Yoshi simply brushes it aside and comes forward like nothing's happened. They trade heavy strikes and after a minute of hard fighting, Yoshi returns to the line, completely at ease. Steve looks calm too, but there are still 29 fights to go.

As he goes through the first few, it's clear Steve's strategy of moving around has gone out of the window. Perhaps his foot is making it too painful. Perhaps his mind has simply switched into forward mode. Either way, Steve is standing his ground and not taking a backward step. He's getting involved with everything that comes his way, punching, kicking and clinching and ground-fighting. He's simply blasting his way through each fight. I wonder how long he can keep it up.

Steve's in control of his earlier fights. He dominates them. But by the time he reaches the middle ranks, he's against some of the stronger brown and black belts, and his strength is beginning to sap. He's taking punishment and losing some of the clinches. One of the brown belts picks him up high and smashes him down hard on the grass. Steve rolls up onto his feet and carries on.

By the time he completes his twentieth fight, it's clear he's not really going to slump any time soon. He's very tired, sure, but still looks as strong as an ox. As he takes a drink and prepares himself for the last ten fighters, I began to wonder how much he'll have left at the end. As usual, I'll be the last fighter, number 30. If Steve is planning a big finish, I'll be his target. I begin to suspect he is.

My fellow black belts do their best to give him a hammering, but Steve is simply too strong to be beaten. He's fighting back hard, taking everything they can throw at him. After 25 fights, Gavin gathered the last five black belts for a quiet word.

'Don't hold back,' he tells us. 'I know Steve is very tired, but this is what he wants and needs. Give him a hard fight, so he can test himself to the limit.'

Mark takes Sensei at his word, and piles into Steve with his explosive combinations, hitting with body shots and smashing low kicks onto the thighs. Steve fights back well and refuses to be overwhelmed.

Now it's Carl's turn. His huge, thudding punches hit with such force, Steve is driven uphill, his face a mask of pain. But he still doesn't look beaten. *After two more hard fights, it's my turn. I jog out to face him. I imagine he has something left in the tank. I haven't guessed quite how much.*

Sensei calls to start and Steve gives a guttural roar and explodes forward, hammering four or five enormous punches onto my chest. The power is incredible, and for a moment, I'm stunned. I'm in danger of being overwhelmed unless I fight back hard, right now.

I switch up a gear and dodge to the left. Though he's still strong, the tiredness is making him a shade too slow to catch me. I cut in and hammer some hard hooks into his body. He hits back. I move out of range and quickly back in.

We exchange punches, toe-to-toe, and soon Steve's tiredness catches up with him. He's been punching for almost half an hour. He pulls me into a clinch to smother my punches. I don't want to wrestle, so I attempt a hip throw, turning in hard. Steve reads it perfectly and counters, dropping his weight and leaning back. He is so strong. I can't force him over and we collapse in a heap.

We stand and slug it out again. Steve draws me into another clinch. I sense he's getting set for a low kick, but I get my knee in first. Now, holding him by the shoulders, I slam my knee into his chest, jerking his arms to keep him off balance. I follow up with two more knees to the body. Steve can't block or cover up. He just takes the blows. I can hear the air being knocked out of him.

His last, ultimate effort has totally exhausted him. Now I can hear his breath coming out in strangled gasps. I've been punching very hard, but now I pull the knee strikes, just a tad. I don't want to break his ribs or crack his sternum.

He comes right back at me. I hit him again with everything I have, body shots, low kicks… again he clinches with me, and I switch back to knees. After three strikes, I attempt another throw, but again he's too strong. I'm forced to let go and roll away.

Soon we're back in the clinch and this time, finally, I succeed in throwing him. Undaunted, he gets up and walks straight back into the fray.

In that minute, I unload everything into him. My strategy is to set a pace that's too fast for him to match, keeping him guessing, switching from punches to kicks to knees to throws, so he has no chance to settle. Still he comes back at me.

The roar of the crowd seems deafening. The fighters in the line-up join in, shouting encouragement to Steve. We lose track of where we are. Finally we stand, punching, toe-to-toe. The roaring in my ears grows even louder and suddenly a dark shape cuts in. It wrestles my opponent to the floor. What's happening?

I realised Gavin has been shouting 'Stop' but we were oblivious. In the end, he's thrown himself between us. Now he's lying on top of Steve, protecting him.

I step back and Gavin gets up. Steve remains on the grass. He gasps up at the sky. He's finished. It's over. The adrenaline is already beginning to fade. Tiredness and pain will soon take over. He seems unable to stand and I step over to help him up, but he's not ready. He resists my help and *stays down a little longer. He's overcome with emotion and turns onto all fours, as if to shut out the world.*

Gavin gives him a few more moments before helping him up. He walks with Steve to our starting point, and we bow. I return to my place in the line-up. I'm breathing hard and my hands are sore. I hit Steve so hard that I bruised my own knuckles.

Steve bows to the line-up and is surrounded by well-wishers. He's overcome with emotion. He's done so much, and come so far for this test. Now it's over. But there will be more pain to come. His injuries will take a long time to heal.

Gavin embraces Steve, and talks to him privately for a minute or two, his hand placed affectionately around Steve's neck. It's a touching sight.

Meanwhile Jay is basking in her own glory. She has also finished the Thirty Man Kumite. To my shame, I barely glanced across to see how she was doing. I'd been too fascinated by Steve's battles. But she's done it, and now she's chatting and joking happily, no doubt eager for her trademark Guinness and cigar, her preferred choice of refreshment.

I'm fascinated by the Thirty Man Kumite. Later by the campfire, I try to talk to Steve and Jay about it. I'm planning to write an article for a karate magazine and I ask for insights from the people at the eye of the storm. They both seem distant, in a world of their own. It's understandable. They're mentally and physically exhausted. I decide to leave them alone and try again tomorrow.

The next day, I brought up the subject again. Neither would elaborate. They'd mutter a few words and retreat into silence. I'd noticed the same thing before, in others who had done the Thirty Man Kumite: Carl, Mark and Charlie. I wondered why.

Normally after a hard grading, there was plenty of banter. Fights would be replayed and everyone would be on a high. Why was the Thirty Man Kumite so different? I would find out soon enough.

Park Life

After an exciting summer camp there's always a buzz in the air for a few weeks. People reflect on their achievements and what they've learned. There's a bit of a high in the dojo. Training is quite light, to let the bruises heal.

Steve's Thirty Man Kumite played on my mind often over those weeks. He'd made a heroic effort and people talked of it often. Again, I began to wonder about doing it myself. Should I ask to attempt it? I weighed up the pros and cons. If I succeeded, it would be an epic achievement, easily the biggest of my martial arts career. It would be one of the biggest things I'd do in my life. Something I would carry with me, always. It would be exciting. I could use everything I'd learned in almost 20 years of karate and put it to the ultimate test. I could make myself into the best fighter I could be, and see how I fared in the hottest flame.

But what if I failed? It would be a disaster. My position as the club's Sempai would become awkward. If I failed, how could I teach people who'd passed? How could I help others prepare if

I couldn't do it myself? I was already 37 years old. I felt fit and technically superior, but I'd never have the boundless energy I had ten years ago.

I remembered how Carl had struggled, aged 37, despite being an exceptional fighter and a natural heavyweight. All three guys who'd done it before had been heavyweights. I was smaller, a middleweight. The batterings they'd taken had been painful to watch. Did I really need that?

In the end, the cons were simply too strong. I pushed all thoughts of the Thirty Man Kumite from my mind. I would concentrate on what I needed as a third dan. I was already an assistant instructor, so I would work on teaching. I'd start practising weapons in earnest. I needed it for my next grading. I decided to throw myself into this instead.

Charmaigne and I began to see her sister and Gavin socially. We'd often go and visit them and even went to Spain together. I found going on holiday with your Sensei has certain drawbacks. While three people are happy to read a novel by the pool, there's always one who wants to climb the jagged mountain range in the distance.

Later, back in London on a sunny afternoon, the phone rang. It was Gavin. There was a short pause. I wondered what he was going to say. Part of me had already guessed. He said he didn't want me to take what he was going to say in the wrong way. That's never a good sign, is it? I steeled myself. He wanted to give me an opportunity, but I wasn't obliged to accept it. He offered to arrange the Thirty Man Kumite for me. The enthusiasm in his voice made it sound like he was doing me a favour. Christ! Did he think I didn't know what was involved?

I thanked him for his most generous offer and explained that I had considered it several times, not least since Steve's inspiring performance. I'd weighed up the pros and cons and decided against it. I gave him my reasons and he seemed to understand. He told me to think it over. The offer still stood. I promised I would, although my mind was made up.

We hung up. I jumped to my feet and began pacing around the room. Damn him, he'd done it now! I was determined not to change my mind. After all, I had considered it rationally and logically and decided against it. I didn't need it. It was a test for second dans and I was already a third dan. It would look like I was being demoted. It would send out the wrong signals to the rest of the club. I was not going to do it.

At the next class I spoke to Gavin again. I reiterated my views, all the reasons for not doing it. He seemed to accept them and nothing more was said. For the next few days, I reassured myself all was well. The offer could be quietly forgotten. Life at the club could go on as normal. But deep down, I knew things would never be the same again. I had turned down a challenge set by my Sensei. I'd never done that before. After a few days, I could bear it no longer. The shame of ducking the challenge was more painful than the thought of doing it.

I began to replay all the good things it would mean. It would be my last chance to push myself to the limit and see what I could really do. The severity of the challenge would force me to train like never before. How far could I go? How good could I get? It had been over ten years since I'd done a serious full-contact competition, but now I was vastly more skilful and experienced. I understood strategy and tactics. I knew how my body worked. I knew how to train properly and condition my mind for success.

Fuck it. I'm going to do it.

I rang Gavin and told him yes.

'Are you sure?' he asked. 'You know this is not a grading for you? You are not required to do it. It's for your own benefit. You're doing it, well, voluntarily…'

I reassured him. 'Yes, I've thought it through. I want to do it. It'll be exciting.'

He was delighted. It was not a grading, so I didn't have to do it at summer camp. He suggested December, after the usual Christmas grading. There would be plenty of higher grades there for me to fight. I accepted. It gave me six months to prepare.

Training began right away. I cut all the crap from my diet and gave up alcohol. I'd have to push myself hard each time I trained. Why make it more difficult than it needed to be? Giving up the beer was a mental sign to myself that I was totally serious about what I was doing.

I decided to follow the example of the best boxers and make running a daily routine. I was living in central London and there was no chance of getting a nice long run in the countryside. I had to make do with the next best thing and jogged over to a football pitch in Shoreditch Park. Here I devised an extended sprint routine for myself.

Although the Thirty Man Kumite seems like a marathon sparring session, I knew it would take just over half an hour. I would be fighting a fresh person every minute, so the intensity of the test would be more of a problem than the duration, more of a middle distance run than a marathon. I didn't want to plod along for hours in my training. I needed to keep up a cracking pace for 30 minutes.

My fitness was already good and I had six months to make it exceptional. There was plenty of time, so my first few sessions weren't too intense. I didn't want to shock my body. It needed time to adjust to the new demands I was going to make of it. For the first six weeks, if I felt too stiff or tired, I would ease off and do a little stretching instead.

I wanted to peak at the right time. Now I was making a long, gentle climb up the foothills. I wanted to reach 'base camp' in good shape. Six weeks before the test, I would strike hard for the summit. During this phase, I would be looking to really hurt myself. In the final week, I would train quite lightly, to allow my body to regain some freshness. On the day itself, I planned to be at my absolute best. Not before. And certainly not after.

Devising the correct training programme is a special skill. The world's top boxers pay a lot of money for the right trainer, someone who really understands what to do. Now was my chance to see how well I could train someone. The difference was, I was the guinea pig. If my ideas failed, I'd be the one paying the price.

In between karate classes, I decided to train alone. There's a lot to be said for training with partners, but I was getting plenty of sparring practice in the dojo. For the rest of the time, I wanted to be my own boss. I didn't need someone yelling at me any more or setting me the wrong exercises. I knew exactly what I wanted to achieve.

I was quite capable of pushing myself to the point of exhaustion. I had all the motivation I needed. It was fear. Not fear of pain. Fear of *failure*. The thought of it scared the hell out me. It was powerful enough to get me out of bed every morning at six and over to the freezing football pitch for training.

Occasionally I was so stiff that I couldn't run properly, so I'd stretch and go home dejectedly. I forced myself to lay off and rest for a day. I'd wait impatiently for my body to recover, so I could throw a few more sessions at it. I didn't want to miss any opportunity to get stronger.

Fitness is built up in thin layers. It grows in the body gradually. It develops in cycles, through work, rest and recovery. First, by exercising, we put our body under more strain than it's used to. We break the muscles down. Then we rest and eat. During this time, the muscles, the heart and lungs, they recover and grow stronger. That's how it works.

There's a delicate balance. Train too little and the muscles won't grow. They only get stronger if they need to. They always do the bare minimum. Train too hard, and the body will take too long to recover. You get a backlash and can't train properly for the next few days. Progress is all about the right ratio of work and recovery.

My training cycles were designed around my working life and my natural bio-rhythms. First thing in the morning I was drowsy and my muscles had contracted overnight. It was not the ideal time to train hard, because I hadn't eaten overnight and my blood sugar was low. But since I had to go to work, I was forced to do my running early.

I'd compensate by drinking a pint of squash, the closest thing to an expensive energy drink. There was no time to have breakfast before running. I would have puked it up again. Eventually my body got used to going from sleep to sprints in a matter of minutes.

At dawn in Shoreditch Park there was an interesting park life going on. I soon became part of it. All the usual characters were there. The fat guy with whiskers and thick glasses, walking his Labrador. He'd stop for a chat and ask what I thought of Bruce Lee and Chuck Norris. Then he'd tell me about his mate who was a tenth dan. *'He'd make mincemeat of you,'* he'd tell me, good-naturedly. I'd humour him for a minute or two and then excuse myself, saying I had to keep working.

There was the man and woman who always let their dogs play together. Perhaps they were having an affair? There was the little old lady with a Yorkie in a red tartan jacket (the dog, not the lady). And of course, there were the hard men with their bulldogs. One guy had a massive Rottweiler that put me on my guard. I was running. I hoped it didn't think I was prey. I clutched my key fob with a long sharp key sticking out, just in case I felt a set of jaws clamping over my leg.

I would warm up for 20 minutes with some basic punches and kicks, before beginning what I called 'The Punisher'. If you've ever tried sprint training, you'll know why. I sprinted back and forth across the football pitch for 30 minutes, mixing in rapid punching and kicking combinations plus press-ups, sit-ups and squats. The idea was to keep myself gasping throughout. This was a cardio session, designed to keep my lungs and legs working at maximum for 30 minutes.

At first, my sprints degenerated into runs and then jogs. But after a few weeks, my body got used to it. My sprints grew faster. I could do 30 minutes without stopping. Then each week, I'd push the intensity to a new level. As the test came closer, I found myself getting seriously good at this routine. One day in the gym I showed off to a friend by setting the running machine to maximum and keeping it there for 20 minutes.

My total training time was always short, little more than an hour. I would warm up and warm down quite gently. My aim was simply to get better and better over 30 minutes, rather than slog away for hours at a sluggish pace. It's not the distance of race that'll kill you, it's the *pace*. I was looking for quality and intensity over 30 minutes, to replicate the test conditions.

After training, I'd wolf down breakfast and rush off to work. I'd eat another bowl of cereal around eleven o'clock, then sandwiches or pasta at lunchtime and fruit and more sandwiches at mid-afternoon. I needed the extra calories to sustain my new work rate. In the evening, I'd train again at the karate club or the gym.

Over the course of a week I'd find my energy levels going through peaks and troughs. Monday was fine, because I'd rest on Sunday. Just a little rusty and reluctant to get going. Tuesday was the best day of the week. I was full of energy. Wednesday was good too. By Thursday, I would begin to flag. Friday was usually a dead loss, so I'd take it easy. This meant I had a little extra energy on Saturday, when I'd do one hard session at midday.

I would use Saturday's session as benchmark, a litmus test for the actual event. As long as I felt a little better each week, I was happy. Once I came to understand this weekly cycle, I went with it, pushing myself hard on key days and training more moderately on others. I tried to make sure I was in good shape for the karate classes, not too tired. I needed to make the most of the sparring that was always on offer.

Once I was feeling stronger and fitter, I began to add mental exercises to my morning sessions. I needed to condition my mind. Before sprinting across the football pitch, I would prowl along the sideline, looking at an imaginary line of 30 fighters. It would stretch almost half the length of the field. I would glare at it malevolently, visualising the faces, catching their eyes. I was going to make each one sorry they had turned up.

At first it seemed absurd to imagine things this way. Outrageously arrogant. Totally unrealistic. But what was my alternative? Ignore it? Pretend it wasn't going to happen? Hope for mercy? I had to tackle the issue head on in my own mind. One day soon, the imaginary line-up would be all too real.

Heavy Bag

My other regular training was bag work. I knew how important it would be for my fitness and conditioning and hunted around for a gym with a good punch bag. I found one near home with a full-length heavy bag hanging in a dance studio. When the aerobics classes finished at eight-thirty the room emptied and I had the place to myself. It was just what I wanted.

I began by moving around and shadow boxing for 15 minutes, stepping, punching, parrying and kicking. Sometimes I added ankle weights and small hand weights. It was very tiring and hard to avoid planting my feet and working from stationary. But the exercise was all about footwork. I gave it another of my names: *Hotflooring*. I didn't allow myself to stand still. I wasn't to know it, but this would prove a vital exercise for me.

As I danced around the studio, doing a poor imitation of the Ali shuffle, I would picture an opponent coming at me. I'd move off at an angle, refusing to accept the exchange on his terms, sidestepping, slipping his punches, circling and attacking from a new angle, hitting and moving before he could turn and face me.

After a few weeks I was moving faster and more gracefully. I could begin to imagine my opponents looking foolish and disorientated as I dazzled them. I enjoyed this idea and tried to cultivate this mental attitude. When I saw myself looking good in the mirrors, I gave myself plenty of mental high fives. I had fun.

Then I would move onto the heavy bag. This was the real training: 30 minutes of bag work, throwing sharp punches and kicks, working on all my combinations. I've always enjoyed the heavy bag. It's a hard task master and unless you hit it with both power and technique, it tends to just hang unmoved, mocking you. Beginners often give it a huge whack only to find it doesn't even move and they injure their hand.

You need to take the time to develop technique before you can reap the rewards. There's something very reassuring about knowing that if push comes to shove, you can bang away with the best of 'em. I'd finish each session with several sets of press-ups, sit-up, squats and stretching.

I'd go to the gym when there was no karate class. The only niggle was I had to wait until eight-thirty before I could get on the bag. This meant hanging around at work, or waiting in the gym. I didn't dare go home. It would be too difficult to go out again.

One evening at eight-thirty the studio was dark. It looked empty. I went in and turned on the light to find one of the gym instructors meditating. She told me I couldn't use the bag until she'd finished.

'How long will that be?' I asked.

'Half an hour,' she answered.

Now this was a problem. The gym would be closing soon and I wouldn't have time to do my whole routine.

'Are you sure I couldn't use it while you're meditating?' I asked, lamely, knowing that someone knocking the living daylights out of a punch bag wasn't going to help her achieve inner peace.

'No, you'll have to wait,' she said brusquely.

In other circumstances, I would have let it go. But now, nothing was allowed to come between me and my training. And she was being a bit out of order. This was a gymnasium, after all, not a temple.

I told her I was sorry but I really needed to train. She told me she was an instructor and she needed the room. I told her I was a paying member and I *really* needed to train. The poor woman didn't understand how badly. In the end, she picked up her mediation mat and stormed out, further from nirvana than ever. Sorry, Missus, but I really, really needed to train.

Over the months, my punches and kicks got harder and meaner. My combinations began to flow. My confidence grew. Then I began to imagine certain fighters in front of me. These were the guys in the line who were going to be trouble. There were four or five that I had in mind. I would picture them one by one as I squared up to the bag. Then they'd get blasted: Bang! Bang! Bang!

This is not an easy admission to make because in karate, we're taught to be respectful to one another at all times. In my defence, I would say this: I never stopped respecting these guys and would count them all as friends, both before, during and after the test. But I knew the hurt they were capable of inflicting on me. I knew they wouldn't be holding back. I felt justified in this approach to help me cope with the difficulties ahead. I expect they do the same, too.

I took heart from the fact I was doing all this extra training while they were relaxing at home. I was getting fit while they were getting fat. I was sprinting across that damn football pitch every morning while they were tucked up in their warm, cosy beds. I was going to make them pay.

Even with all my positive mental preparations, a little bit of dread would creep into my mind every now and then. When it did, I would force myself to think past the test to the moment I completed it successfully. It was going to be a fantastic feeling. We'd all go for a curry and re-run the fights, compare bruises and retire to the pub, where I'd enjoy a few well-earned pints. Christmas was going to be especially fine this year. I'd be able to totally slob out and relax without a care in the world.

Soon I felt myself getting stronger and fitter than ever before. I began to feel very confident in my ability. One evening after a bag work session where I felt on top of the world, I asked

Charmaigne a very pointed question: If everyone in the line-up tried their best to take me out, did she think I could withstand it? She hesitated, then told me gently that in all honesty, nobody could survive in those circumstances. I told her I disagreed and felt ready to give them all a lesson they would never forget.

Hard Sparring

I attended every karate class without fail. I learned long ago never to skip classes, even if it's to train on something more specific. It's never quite the same. If you're away for a week or more, it can be quite hard to walk back through the door. Just being in the dojo, doing karate, keeps everything familiar. You feel you belong. When you step up for a hard test, you have a sense of security that you can't get any other way.

Sensei Gavin obliged me with plenty of hard sparring in the months leading up to the test. This was just what I wanted. With so many high grades at the club, there was never any shortage of quality sparring partners.

Often I would go toe-to-toe with some of the big hitters, allowing them to kick and punch me with minimal resistance. I wanted to get used to being in the thick of it and riding the blows. This is a fine art, not to be confused with taking a beating. In full-contact fights you can't expect to block or evade everything. Being hit is inevitable, but you can diminish the effects in a couple of ways. The first is to breath out at the moment of impact. This tenses your muscles and expels the air from your lungs, so you don't get winded. The second is to move *with* the strike, so you're not absorbing the full impact. I knew when I got tired, I would not be able to dance away from everything. I needed to get used to getting hit without being incapacitated.

With the light, fast fighters at the club I would try to match them for speed without resorting to strength. There's little point in practising 'banging' on small people and dancing away from slow people. You learn nothing. But if you try it the other way around, it forces you to get better.

I tried to spar with people on their terms, forcing myself to adapt to their style. I wanted to practise coping with all forms of attack. If I'm stronger than someone, I can beat them into submission, but what do I learn? If I let a weaker opponent open up on me and attack hard without fear of retaliation, I always get something to practise against. I already have my own style. I know what I can do. It's the other person I'm worried about. What are *they* going do?

This is only in friendly sparring. When it comes to a competitive match, I'll want the fight on my terms and do everything to prevent my opponent doing what he does best.

I chose my sparring partners carefully. If I was tired, I'd avoid the fiercest fighters. I didn't want to risk being overpowered and having my confidence dented. When I felt good, I made sure to face them and give them some stick. This way I reassured myself they could not dominate me.

It was important to face my fears in advance. All of them. I didn't want any nasty surprises on the day. I forced myself to imagine the worst possible line-up. All the best fighters would be there. Gavin and Dan might bring in some ringers from outside, or join in themselves. It was unlikely, but I pictured it nonetheless, to avoid being unnerved. Whatever they did, it would be no big deal. I was up for it.

Some of the guys at the club were surprised to hear I was attempting the Thirty Man Kumite. It wasn't a grading for me. What would I gain from it? There wasn't enough time for a full explanation – they'll have to read the book – so 'just for fun' seemed as good an answer as any. They laughed, but it was a strange time. We all knew they'd be trying to knock the crap out of me in a few weeks' time.

The pressure began to mount and I found myself entering a new state of mind, a form of mental tunnel vision. All my attention was on training. I thought of little else. Fortunately, I knew this would happen and talked to Charmaigne about it. I said I'd be acting a little strange over the next few months and asked her to bear with me.

I felt myself becoming more and more aggressive. I was ready to argue with anyone and grew impatient with people around me. I had to make a special effort to stay calm at work. I couldn't afford to be rude to people, especially as a freelancer.

My eating habits became a standing joke. My clients kept boxes of cereal for staff and the boss told me to help myself, but I ate so much it became embarrassing. In the end I had to bring in my own box of Fruit and Fibre.

Six weeks before the test I decided I'd reached base camp in good shape. It was time to strike hard for the summit. I turned up the intensity of my sessions and pushed myself to new heights. It hurt. But not as much as it was going to hurt the day I reached the top.

Christmas was fast approaching. I was invited to several office parties and the karate club had its own bash. I went along but I was poor company, sipping on an orange juice and checking my watch for the first chance to slip away. I was only interested in one thing: getting a good night's sleep so I could train hard the next morning.

I was terrified of getting an injury that would interrupt my training. I remember walking very deliberately on the pavement to avoid twisting my ankle. Everything went according to plan, until the final week. On my last gym session, I felt a pain in my lower back. It came from no particular exercise. My body had simply done too much. It gave way at my weakest point, which has always been my back.

The stiffness got gradually worse. The next day I was hobbling around like an old man. Physically it wasn't a big problem, because I was going to train very light in the last week. The niggle would probably be gone by the day of the test. But mentally, it was a different story. I'd wanted to be feeling great, full of energy and raring to go. Now my body felt like a wreck. Two trips to the physio made a difference and I managed to do a little gentle training to keep from stagnating.

By the day of the Thirty Man Kumite the pain was almost gone. I'd intended to do a gentle warm-up that morning, but my injury still worried me. I didn't want to risk making it worse, so I spent the day prowling around the flat or lying on the carpet with my feet on the sofa.

I found myself strangely calm, not in the least bit nervous. I was totally in 'the zone', far more confident than I'd been for other, easier tests in the past. I knew I was fully prepared. Although my back was niggling me, I knew I was amazingly fit. I was eager to show everyone what I could do. I wanted to get it on. And get it over with.

Waking Dragons

Sunday 15 December 2002 is a day I won't forget in a hurry. I had focused on it for six months of my life. It was the day of the Thirty Man Kumite.

Late in the afternoon I drove along the Marylebone Road and up the A5 to Kilburn. Thankfully, traffic was light. The last thing I wanted was to be stuck in a jam. Charmaigne was quiet in the car, wisely leaving me to my own thoughts. When we got to the aptly named Shoot Up Hill we turned off and parked near the dojo. The normal grading had just finished and the place was full, noisy and buzzing.

There were high grades everywhere. They had come from all over the country to fight me. There were five from Bristol, one from Portsmouth and one had even flown in from Holland. Mark had come up from Devon. Carl had come down from Cambridge.

I was flattered. I was also relieved to see so many people. I wanted my Thirty Man Kumite to be a good one. I wanted no question that my line-up was easier than anyone else's. Also, I didn't want to have to fight the same people twice. There's something satisfying about getting a difficult fighter out of the way and moving on.

Among all the familiar faces, I spotted one that seemed out of place. I realised it was the Sempai from my previous club at Curtain Road, a third dan black belt. One of my buddies had persuaded him to come and join in. It was great to see him after several years and we spoke warmly for while, until it was time to get changed and prepare.

I went upstairs to a room that had been set aside for me and another guy who was also attempting the Thirty Man Kumite that day. As we got changed, I assessed myself. How did I feel? Physically, I felt good, just a slight stiffness in my back. I knew it would disappear as soon as I got warm. Mentally, I felt good too. I was not the least bit nervous. I was excited. I was part of a great ceremony. We were all participating in something special. I was just the focal point.

Looking down from the balcony, I could see a long line of people forming. There was no one who would be considered a pushover. But towards the end of the line-up, I noticed four black belt women. Charmaigne wasn't one of them. Gavin must have felt the conflict of interest would be too much and she got the job of timekeeper instead.

I was a bit perturbed to see women in my line-up. I didn't want people to say it was easy. I was a bit worried about hurting them, although they were all tough fighters and capable of taking care of themselves. I shrugged off the worry. I'd prepared for the worst. Now things seemed to be getting easier. I was eager to go down there and get the proceedings under way.

I went over my strategy once again. In previous tests, some of the guys had sent out a stern warning early on. This can make the rest of the line-up fight more carefully, or it can backfire and make people go in harder. I had a different plan. I was going to coast through the early fights, dancing out of trouble and giving them a sparring lesson along the way. When I got to the middle, I would increase my work rate. Finally, I'd end with some great fights with the highest grades.

I warmed up in the little changing room and kept this plan in my mind. I laughed and joked with my companion until he was called down to begin his line-up. He was going first. Once he'd completed ten fights, I'd start along the same line-up. We'd fight at the same time for a while, until he'd finished. Then I'd do my last ten fights on my own.

As usual, there was no great ceremony. After a quick bow, he began. I didn't want to watch his fights too closely. I didn't want to get too excited or nervous. But I was keen to assess the mood of the line-up, so I glanced over from time to time.

What I saw shocked me. The level of contact was very severe. The opening fighters were hyped up. The whole association was watching and they didn't want to look soft. They were hitting with real intent. The sound of each kick and punch echoed around the dojo's high ceiling with a sharp *crack*.

By the fifth fight, my friend took a nasty punch in the midsection which knocked him over. He got up and continued, but the seriousness of the test was beginning to dawn on him. He was breathing heavily by now, and showing signs of tiring. Body shots and low kicks were raining down on him thick and fast.

I brushed this worrying sight from my mind and went back inside the changing room. I had to concentrate on my own fights. I shadow-boxed lightly to get warm and consoled myself with the thought that in an hour's time, it would all be over. In two hours time, I'd be in the pub, basking in glory.

After ten fights, my friend got a short break and I joined him on the mat. I was still buoyant. As I bowed to the line-up, I was grinning inanely, winking and smirking at people. But once I got started, reality soon hit.

My first fight was against a friend who I'd introduced to karate a few years earlier. He'd been a little out of shape and a bit uncoordinated, but he'd trained religiously. I'd often trained with him to help him. Now my good deeds were being punished.

He lunged forward strongly, attacking me with hard two-punch combinations. I slipped to the side to avoid him and hit back skilfully, but I took several heavy strikes. If this was my friend, what could I expect from my enemies?

The second fighter was one of those thin, bony people that hurt when you clashed. We exchanged punches and kicks. As I moved out again, he spun around and hit me on the nose with a backfist strike. The face wasn't supposed to be a target, but no one stopped the fight. No one seemed to care! It made my vision cloud up and I had trouble focusing. The rest of the fight was a blur.

In the third fight, after a furious exchange, I found myself in a clinch. I was locked together with my opponent. I wanted to avoid wrestling because it's so tiring, but I was already getting tied up. I made a half-hearted attempt at a throw, hoping to conserve my energy. It lacked commitment and I got thrown myself. As I rolled to my feet the truth began to dawn. The test was going to be so much more difficult than I'd imagined.

The next fighter attacked me with a wild look in his eyes, throwing low kicks that would cripple me if they connected. I found this aggression difficult to come to terms with. I tried to hit back calmly and avoid the worst of the strikes. I didn't want to get involved in a big tear-up early on. I was planning to save that for the end.

The fifth fight was fast and furious. My arms and legs were beginning to lose their spring. The sheer effort of the struggle was sapping my energy fast, and I could only just match my opponent. I was taking a lot more hits.

Half way through the sixth fight, I heard the loud call of 'Yame!' We stopped. I looked over to see what the problem was. The other chap who was attempting the Thirty Man Kumite had been knocked out. He couldn't carry on. Sensei Gavin gave him a short examination and announced that he would be retiring. The line-up bowed to him and he sat to the side. It had been his sixteenth fight.

Now the full enormity of my situation struck me. I was only on my sixth fight and feeling very tired. These were supposed to be the easier fights. What had gone wrong? I looked at the huge line-up of fighters still to come. It coiled around three sides of the mat like some great white dragon waiting to devour me, and suddenly the task ahead seemed impossible.

I burned with annoyance at myself. Why was I feeling so weak? Obviously I had not trained hard enough. Or perhaps the guys who'd succeeded before were simply so much better than me? I'd been a fool to even contemplate the Thirty Man Kumite.

What could I do to get out of this frightful predicament? One word to Sensei would be enough to extricate myself. But the shame of giving up like that would be unbearable. I realised I'd have to fight on until I too was unable to continue. I pictured myself being carried off the mat and into an ambulance on a little red stretcher. Then Sensei shouted for the fight to continue.

My seventh fight was against a powerful fighter from Bristol who stalked me before unleashing huge, devastating low kicks and body shots. I fought back, doing my best to avoid a direct hit. When I caught him with a spinning back kick, he simply trapped my leg and swept me hard to the ground. I got back to my feet, exhausted. By the end of this fight, in just seven minutes, I was totally spent.

Now I lost count of what fight I was on. I clung to the idea of reaching the tenth fight when I would get a short break. I told myself it couldn't be far off. The next fighter came out strongly, forcing me backwards. He smiled as I hit him. My punches seemed to have no effect.

When a minute was called, I felt I'd been given one more chance. Convinced it was the tenth fight, I rode the wave as another powerful fighter piled into me. As soon as we finished, yet another fighter squared up. I realised there was one more to go. I hung on for grim death. One spectator told me afterwards she noticed the colour drain from my face. I was at my lowest ebb.

Finally, my break came. I took a sip of my drink and assessed the situation. I felt sick. I was disgusted with myself. I had not prepared enough. I had underestimated the task and the fighters. Now I was going to be humiliated in front of so many people.

I was trapped. I'd wandered into a dark cavern and woken a huge beast from its slumber. There was no going back. No surrender. No choice but to fight on until I was torn apart.

I resisted the temptation to sit or kneel. I paced up and down angrily, fighting to regain some composure in front of all these people. I looked over to see who was next in the line-up. It was what someone later described hilariously as the Axis of Evil – three of the strongest, most talented young fighters in the association. They were always a real handful. Now they were waiting for me in a neat row.

With ten seconds to go, I felt a little colour return to my cheeks. I did what I could to help myself. I clapped my hands and whooped to hype myself up. The audience responded with a loud cheer. They were giving me great support. I felt a warm feeling of gratitude to them and a small rush of adrenaline.

Could I make anything of this? As I walked back to the centre of the mat, I remembered the importance of mental attitude. I needed a new scenario to believe in. A new way to encourage myself. Plan A had clearly failed. There was no way I was going to dazzle these guys with my footwork or beat them into submission. But through the fog, Plan B began to form. I had to force myself to survive.

Failure would be terribly humiliating. I was already a recognised third dan. People had assumed I was capable of the test. To fail would not only expose me but also put my Sensei's judgement into question and throw the entire grading structure into confusion. This was all extra pressure on me, but I wondered if I could turn it to my advantage. As a third dan, I also felt entitled to certain liberties. So I began to use the crowd.

Normally I try to cut them out and ignore their silly suggestions. But this time was different. They were all friends and they were making a big noise for me. I decided to tap into this energy and use my feeling of obligation to the club to my advantage.

I held my hand up to my ear. *I can't hear you,* I motioned. They cheered louder. I raised my hands, as if to say *louder still* and they went wild. This gave me a rush that I badly needed. It renewed the impossibility of giving up. I couldn't make such a public show of confidence and then fold. Like Cortes burning his boats after landing in the New World, I was making a public declaration that I was going to do something. There would be no turning back.

Fight 11 began. He seemed a foot taller than me and he was frighteningly fast. Normally I'd move fast to keep out of his long range, but I was too tired. I fought in close, doing my best to slip his punches and his fast front kick and land some of my own. A nasty kick got past my guard and slammed into my gut. I felt sick. I moved off to avoid the follow-up punches. I hit back. When a couple of my shots landed, I felt a certain satisfaction. Then two more hard punches got through and winded me again. I tried not to show it. Soon a minute was up and the next guy came out.

He was another of the club's most feared fighters. He stepped forward into his usual poised stance, stalking and then unleashing withering combinations. I saw a tremendous low kick coming and raised my leg to block. The kick came so low, it swept my blocking leg aside and hit my supporting leg. I stumbled, struggling to stay on my feet. Another low kick caught me hard in the centre of the thigh. This was getting dangerous. People in the line-up began shouting to me: *'It's time to move!'* Normally they tease me about moving too much, but now I was drained. But they were right.

I forced myself to shift, switching my stance to protect my battered leg. I began to operate a programme of 'damage management'. When I took a big hit in one place, I guarded it carefully to make sure I didn't take another in the same place. At least for a while. You can usually take one good shot, but if you take three or four in exactly the same spot, it will undo you. You'll collapse.

By keeping the damage peppered evenly over my body, I found I could keep going. I managed to block or slip most of the techniques, but three or four hard strikes were getting through in each fight. I became resigned to this, and simply made sure they weren't in the same place twice.

Fight 13 was the last of the Axis of Evil. My opponent was a wonderful fighter, very dangerous, but he knew I was hurting and eased off slightly. As our fight came to an end, a new fact dawned on me. I had survived the Axis of Evil, relatively unscathed. If I could hang on and continue this way, maybe I could do a few more fights. Perhaps I could even get to twenty?

The next two fights were hard work, tough but uneventful. Fight 16 was going to be interesting. I knew the guy was taking no prisoners tonight. I'd seen the way he'd laid into my friend earlier on. Still, by the time we squared up, I was not too worried. I had faced him many times before, in my mind. This was just another fight. As soon we began, he drove me back with a barrage of heavy punches. I felt myself backed up against a wall. Alarm bells rang in my head. I darted to the side before he could really open up. I knew he would take me out there and then if I wasn't careful.

I refused to let him. I headed for the centre of the mat, where he couldn't trap and pummel me. He drove me backwards with his relentless attacks. I blocked and moved as best I could. Eventually, I was cornered again and the punches began to land hard. I knew I was in trouble, and the bile rose in my stomach. I had to get out of the corner. With a big effort I darted to the side and turned him.

Now I was backing away towards the centre of the mat again, but I wanted show him that he hadn't hurt me. I summoned some extra energy and caught him with a spinning back kick. It wasn't hard enough to hurt him, but it felt good to me. That was all that mattered.

Unconcerned, he cornered me again and began pummelling. Again I slipped away and in a final act of defiance, I caught him with the same spinning kick a second time. In the far reaches of my mind I could hear the crowd going wild, but he was already on top of me again. He cornered me for the final ten seconds and beat me unmercifully. Then the minute was up, and he had to stop. I'd got through.

This fight had exhausted me, so I confess to feeling relieved when the next fighter was the first of the girls. I decided to take it easy and catch my breath. It was not to be. Soon her blows were coming through so hard, I felt myself beginning to waiver.

'You can hit her back!' shouted Charmaigne from the sidelines, thinking perhaps I was holding back out of gentlemanly concern. This wasn't the case, I was simply spent. But I realised the accumulation of punches might knock me down if I didn't stop them. I hit her with a few kicks and punches of my own, cursing myself for forgetting that the women in the club have always been a force to be reckoned with.

I clung to the idea of reaching fight 20, where I would get another break. I fought another girl, whose strikes were equally hard. Then a big strong lad came out to face me. He remembered me giving him a kicking in his black belt grading and came at me with a barrage of punches and kicks that drove me back steadily. There was a lopsided grin on his face the whole time.

How the tables had turned. Now I was facing all the guys I'd been happily battering when they were knackered. This was their one chance to pay me back and they were taking it with glee. Oh well, you reap what you sow.

The next fighter darted in and out quickly, hitting me almost at will. I struck out whenever I could but my movements were slow and ponderous. My limbs were too heavy. I seemed to be operating in a different time frame. My body was taking a serious pounding. I brought my hands down to cover my ribs and took a kick to the head. For a moment, I was glad to take a blow to a new, undamaged part of me. Then I chided myself. How could I be so stupid? A head kick could easily knock me out if I wasn't careful, and that would be disastrous. I kept my hands up and fought on.

Finally I finished 20 fights. My second and last break was called. I stood at the side of the mat, flushed and dazed, sipping a drink and glaring around me. I had two minutes to compose myself before the last ten fights. I took stock of the situation.

I felt different now. Something inside me had changed. Physically I was exhausted. But mentally, I was far stronger. I went over all the things I'd accomplished so far: the months of hard training, the 20 fights I'd just done, the danger-spots in the line-up that I'd passed. And I decided one thing for certain. I was going to get it over with, right here, right now. I never wanted to go through any of it again.

I prowled up and down the edge of the mat, steeling myself for the task ahead. Sensei Gavin walked by and muttered under his breath.

'All right?'

'Fine,' I nodded.

Then I gave myself another mental jolt. Another form of boat-burning.

'Don't pull me out, whatever happens,' I told him.

He assured me he wouldn't.

Normally I hate bravado and would have been deeply embarrassed to say that. It's like a line from a naff movie script. But now I needed every edge I could get. I needed to give myself no option but to continue.

This was where many years of karate conditioning came to the fore. I don't mean physical conditioning, though of course that helps. I mean mental conditioning. From my first lesson I'd been told to stand up straight, keep myself tidy and avoid leaning on the wall or slopping on the floor. This wasn't out of some petty need for manners and decorum. It has a vital fighting application. I had to convince my opponents, and myself, that I was far from beaten.

So I rejected the idea of sitting or kneeling. It would be an admission that I was tired. I was all too aware of the work I had left to do. The next ten fighters were the highest grades in the association. There were at least two very big fights to get through.

I walked back onto the centre of the mat, encouraging the crowd to cheer louder. They made another great noise for me.

As I began my twenty-first fight, I felt my mind clearing. I was beginning to take some control of my situation. I could see light at the end of the tunnel.

My opponent was another old friend who I'd coached in the past. Now, with no respect or gratitude for his friend and Sempai, he piled into me with stiff, hard punches and kicks that were hurting like hell. Unable to match his energy, I began hitting back with a different aim in mind. I timed my punches and kicks to land just as he was preparing to strike, to un-weight him and foil his attacks. It worked, most of the time. It was just enough to stop him really opening up on me, but every so often, a hard shot would get through.

I noticed his face was contorted with concentration. He was taking his task of Sempai-bashing very seriously. So I took another liberty and whispered to him 'relax.' It's what I've always told him in the dojo and we laughed. The tension was broken for an instance. Then we carried on as before. Anything to keep my mind off the pain.

The next few fights went by very quickly. One after another, the black belts came out to give me an expert bashing. But after so much practice I had become adept at coping with their attacks. I did my best to conserve a little energy for fight 27, which I knew would be a tough one. I knew Mark was waiting for me, near the end of the line. I'd roughed him up at the end of his test. He was sure to return the favour.

After several more gruelling fights, the time came to face him. He stood before me and bowed with a small smile on his face. Sensei shouted '*Hajime!*' and Mark took a small step forward, raising his guard nonchalantly. This was his style. I knew he would stalk me, even allow me a few shots, before unleashing awful retribution. But I'd fought him so many time in my head, I was completely prepared.

He let me catch him with a few tentative strikes, just as I'd imagined, then exploded into me with vicious punches. He grabbed hold and launched knee strikes into my chest. I raised my game to survive the whirlwind and broke loose. I tried my new tactic of striking just before he attacked to keep the pressure off, but Mark was too good. He simply brushed my punches aside and piled in with fists and knees. Now I was cornered and the strikes were raining in on me. With another huge effort I broke away, hitting and moving to avoid a beating that could finish me off.

Mark backed me into a corner again. I slipped to the side but my back hit the wall. Then an accidental punch caught me square on the jaw. It was hard. But I realised an important fact: if I was registering anything, I wasn't unconscious. It hadn't knocked me out. There was no need to go down. I brushed it off and continued.

This thought process happened in a split second. Sensei Gavin inquired if I was OK and I waved the fight on. Mark touched my face in apology and then continued his assault. It may sound strange, but I remember enjoying the feeling of tangling at such a high level.

We fought for a few more seconds, then 'time' was called. It was over. I was very pleased with myself. I'd weathered one of the biggest storms of the line-up.

This thrilling fight had left me very tired and the next two were hard work. The Sempai from my old club was up next. He swept me easily. I simply rolled back onto my feet and continued. I was fighting on autopilot. My mouth was bloody and hanging open. I was drenched in sweat. I knew I looked a mess. But inside, I was totally calm. I knew the end was in sight.

Fight 29 came. I fought another old friend who traded punches and kicks happily with me. I did my best to conserve one last ounce of energy for the last fight. A minute later, that time had finally come.

The crowd roared huge support for me. I tidied myself up and prepared for one final, enormous effort. Then I saw something I'd imagined many times before. Carl was standing before me. It was a very special moment.

Carl had been one of my first seniors, almost twenty years ago. He'd helped us to train for knockdown and had been an inspiration to us all. He'd also been the first person I'd seen complete the Thirty Man Kumite, at the ripe old age of 37, and he'd led the way for me to do the same. On that hot afternoon two years ago in the campsite near Portishead, I'd been his last fight and we'd had one to remember. Now here he was, ready to repay the kindness.

We bowed. He shouted loudly and stepped forward strongly. I put my guard up one last time. His power drove me straight into a corner. I tried to fight my way out but enormous heavy blows caught me in the ribs, stomach, arms, chest, legs. I hit back, but my limbs weren't working properly. My footwork, once so fast and graceful, was reduced to a few plodding steps. Just enough to keep me moving.

I launched a few counters. I was determined not to let him have it all his own way. I threw punches and low kicks, taking care to keep my guard high. I knew Carl's kicks could take my head off at any moment – they were so heavy, even a playful 'tap' could knock me out. I'd seen it happen during friendly sparring.

But Carl wasn't trying to knock me out. He was just giving me one final stuffing for good measure. Something for me to battle against. It felt good to be fighting at this level. I hit back as strongly as I could. He caught me again and again with massive punches and kicks. I was proud to be standing up to him after so many fights. And while I was hurting, I was in no danger of defeat. My spirits were up. My pilot light was burning bright inside me and there was no stopping me.

Carl cornered me once more and hammered away. I stumbled into the line-up and Sensei shouted '*Yame!*' to stop the fight. I thought it must be over. So did everyone else. The crowd went wild, letting out a huge cheer. Some began thumping the mat with their fists, until the whole dojo shook. But I felt nothing. No relief. No joy. I was far away.

Sensei shouted that there were ten seconds left on the clock. Again I felt nothing. No annoyance. No despair. Carl and I simply squared up and carried on. I was beyond tiredness and beyond worry. I'd reached a happy place where I simply didn't mind any more.

Time was called, and now it really was over. I still didn't care. No particular thoughts or feelings ran through my mind. I was miles away.

I took a formal bow to the line-up and people swarmed around to congratulate me. Charmaigne ran over to hug me. I still felt very distant. It took a while for me to come around. Then I began talking and smiling with my friends. I embraced some of the fighters and shook their hands. There was a warm buzz about the place and the tension quickly melted away.

Aftermath

I was always been struck by the silence surrounding the Thirty Man Kumite. The people who'd done it never wanted to talk about it. Now I knew why. Even for a seasoned fighter, it's a traumatic experience. You can't control the line-up. You can't *beat* it. The beast is far too powerful.

As you wrestle with it, terrible thoughts run through your head: *Am I going to fail, in front of all these people?* You are exposed. Your character is held up for public scrutiny. Your soul is bared to the world. Completing the test is not an excuse for triumphant celebrations. It's a moment of humility. The dragon has held you in its jaws, toyed with you to see what you were made of, and the spat you back out again.

It's not uncommon for fighters to break down with emotion after the Thirty Man Kumite and suffer depression afterwards. Perhaps it's a mild form of post-traumatic stress disorder. The fighting is stressful enough, but it's just the end of a long, slow build-up of tension that starts months in advance.

Later when Steve wrote about his Thirty Man Kumite, I wasn't surprised that he came to similar conclusions. It's the public nature of the test that makes it so hard. The spotlight is on you the entire time. You're alone. There's no group to hide behind, no team to feel part of, nothing to distract the attention of the crowd or the instructors.

This encourages your opponents to fight harder. Their performance is under scrutiny too. So the pace is hard from the very start. Like me, Steve had felt very tired after his opening few fights and wondered how he was going to get through. Then much later, he'd realised he was going to succeed.

I spoke privately with Gavin at the edge of the mat. He asked me how I felt. I told him I'd done everything wrong. My strategy had been flawed. Hopelessly naïve. My training hadn't worked. Instead of putting in a mercurial performance, I'd been forced to abandon my game plan almost immediately and just try to survive. I'd been bumping along the bottom the entire the time. I was deeply disappointed in myself.

Then he shone a little light on the matter for me.

'That's the test,' he explained. 'It's not a physical test. It's mental. The training you did was just your entry ticket. It gave you the means to get through, but not the will. That had to come from somewhere else.'

I wondered if he was right? I needed time to think about it.

I made my way upstairs to the changing room on stiff, battered legs. Charmaigne helped me out of my sweat-soaked gi and we checked my body. I was covered in ugly purple bruises and red, raw welts. There was a lump on my shin the size of a tennis ball. She covered it with ice-spray and rubbed arnica cream into my bruised hands and arms. I got changed and we went out into the cold night air.

A big group came with us to the local Tandoori and then on to the North London Tavern, where I rewarded myself with a few well-earned pints. By this time my energy had returned and I was buzzing and hyper, talking to everyone about the test. The humility didn't last long in my case, did it?

Later, we gave Sensei Gavin a lift home. Charmaigne drove. As he got out of the car, Gavin told me he was pleased with my performance. From him, these words meant a lot. I was glad he was pleased. But I was still not happy myself.

At home, I ran a hot bath and eased myself into the kneeling position, letting the hot water relax my battered thighs. Then I lay back and reflected on the whole experience. I wasn't quite sure what to make of it.

After a few minutes in the hot water, I felt very sick. Four pints of Guinness and a curry are not the best cure for being punched repeatedly in the stomach. I got out and stumbled into bed and into a deep sleep.

I'd taken the precaution of booking two days off work to recover. I knew my body would be a wreck. The next morning, I ran another bath and lounged around at home, enjoying the stillness and lack of pressure. All in all, I wasn't too badly hurt. My swollen shin had returned to a more normal size. There were no serious injuries. Just tired muscles and nasty bruises.

I got hold of a video of the event and settled down to watch it. It had been filmed from the balcony, where I'd first looked down onto my line-up. Shot from up there, the whole thing seemed calm and distant. The sound of the punches and kicks seemed more muted than the harsh 'crack' I'd heard and felt in real life.

Watching myself was strange. I was surprised at how calm I appeared. I fought the whole line-up poker-faced. I moved tidily for the most part. Even when I was exhausted, I was never too ragged. When I spoke to people who'd been there, they seemed to have the same view. They told me I'd made it look quite easy. I'd ridden the storm calmly. While it wasn't the most exciting Thirty Man Kumite, it was certainly one of the most composed.

This was completely at odds with the way I'd been feeling inside. My mind had been racing this way and that. Thoughts of doubt and despair had been assailing me, especially early on, along with anger, frustration and fear. I'd been terrified of failing. For a good part of the event, it was the only thing keeping me going. Fear has its uses.

I wondered about my training and my mental preparations. Had I done enough? I couldn't imagine how I could have trained harder. My fitness had been correct, too. I'd done the work I needed for the job. I'd managed to keep moving, albeit far more slowly than I'd hoped, throughout the test. These small movements had prevented me taking the full force of the strikes. I had ridden the blows instead of being hit like a sitting duck.

Had I gone overboard with my mental preparations? I remembered telling Charmaigne I could beat the whole line-up, and she told me it was impossible. Yes, it had been naïve. But looking back, I'm not convinced it was wrong. I'd seen how tough the Thirty Man Kumite could be. I'd hated the idea of taking a beating, so I'd done the only thing possible. I'd convinced myself I would be the one inflicting it instead.

This hadn't happened, but I'd carried the internal conviction that I was *capable* of doing so. I'd never considered myself inferior to any fighter in front of me. This inner belief had proved vital when the pressure got intense.

The truth of what Gavin told me dawned on me. My hard training *had* given me the fitness I'd needed to get through. But when things got ugly, my *mind* had been filled with doubt. For a while, I'd found myself in a dark place. But eventually I'd managed to lead myself out. And that was the test.

Once I'd got into a routine, my mind had settled and I'd felt quite serene. Instead of worrying about the future, I'd become centred in what I was doing, in the *present*. I'd been in harmony with my line-up and fought naturally and instinctively. I'd reached a state of *Mushin* (no mind). It's not the same as mindless. It just means total immersion in the task, without the distraction of other thoughts or emotions.

I'd discovered a level of resolve I didn't know I possessed. I'd never needed it before. It had taken the Thirty Man Kumite to bring it out. When my physical power had drained away, frighteningly quickly, my spirit had stepped in and taken over. These are highly prized experiences for a martial artist. The test made them possible for me.

The line-up proved an interesting animal. A beast with a mind of its own. It had been capable of breaking me, but that was not its aim. It just wanted to see what I was made of. The real surprise was that its expectations had been so much higher than my own. It had forced me to fight so much harder than I could have imagined possible.

I felt a deep bond with my line-up, a sense of kinship which I still feel today. I can remember the fights and the fighters quite clearly. I'm glad they pushed me the way they did. It would have been easy for them to lay off me, but the bastards didn't hold back.

With their help, I'd gone way beyond my previous achievements. It had been far from spectacular and by no means unique, but I'd fought 30 people in a row, full contact, and lived to tell the tale. Now I could drop it into any conversation whenever I liked (ever so casually, of course).

The test was the culmination of all my years of training with excellent instructors, and fellow students, who had sweated alongside me and kept me working hard.

My beginnings in judo had given me a great grounding in fitness, balance, timing and mental attitude. When I switched to karate as a young man, I picked up the training very easily.

Sensei Claronino and Kyokushinkai gave me one of the best starts you could ask for in karate: plenty of hard training, simple, technical excellence and the cultivation of a strong spirit. I'd learned to fight in the hard, uncompromising Knockdown style needed for the Thirty Man Kumite. Though I moved onto other arts, his teachings always stayed with me.

Studying taekwondo with Stav taught me to relax between the hard exchanges of punches and kicks. I learned to conserve my energy and use it more efficiently, avoiding tightening up and slowing down.

My years of Japanese Goju Ryu with Shihan Rowen taught me precision and fluidity, correct posture and balance. I'd leaned to place every footstep just 'so', ensuring I was always in a position to attack or defend, never wrong-footed or off balance. I learned *Zanshin* (awareness) which helped me keep my head during the test, my eyes open, my mind on the job. I didn't 'lose it' or get disorientated, not for an instant, even when I got punched hard in the face or badly winded.

And Sensei Gavin? Well, he allowed all my past styles to come together naturally into his own brand of Okinawan Goju Ryu, also called 'combat karate'. He never tried to undo what I'd learned before. He simply built on it and added to it. He made me a more complete fighter than ever before. And he gave me a gift, albeit a rather hideous one, by getting me to face the Thirty Man Kumite.

It was a gift because every test counts for something. Every hard lesson, tough grading or tournament that we put behind us makes us stronger. Every new challenge faced leaves us with new knowledge, understanding, experience and self-belief. These are some of life's most precious commodities.

The harder the test, the greater the reward. Gavin didn't need to set me the challenge, but he did anyway and I'm grateful. Now the rewards are mine to keep.

I remember feeling, as a young man, that martial arts would be so much more enjoyable if it wasn't for the nerves. The fighting was exciting, almost fun, but the pre-fight nerves were always excruciating.

Today I understand these are the real battles. We win or lose our matches against our opponents according to the will of the Tao. But victory over inner demons depend only on our own will. The conquest of fear is the true reward.

This should come as no surprise. It has always been the stated aim of karate masters to forge a good character and a strong spirit in the student. Fitness and self-defence are valuable by-products, but they are not the underlying reason for training.

Very few martial artists are professional fighters or security staff. Most are people like you and me, studying martial arts for no discernable end or reason. It's just something for the soul. This is art. Art doesn't need to have meaning or express ideas to others. The simple act of doing it is its own reward.

It makes us feel alive. Dancers love to dance. Painters love to paint. Musicians love to play.

Masters talk of karate-do, the 'way' of karate. It isn't something you do on Monday and Thursday evenings. It's a daily ritual, a passion, a way of life. The character and spirit forged in the dojo seeps through into daily life, and helps us tread the correct path at home, at work and among our fellow human beings.

There are no special powers that enable martial artists to perform spectacular feats. What the public sees as amazing comes from innumerable hours of training. All you need is the determination to keep training hard enough, for long enough. Nothing more. As Sensei Gavin likes to say: *'The secret of training is training.'*

This may seem obvious, but you'd be surprised. So many people waste so much time searching for an easier option. A new art. A shorter path to black belt. A new health drink with a secret ingredient. This is mostly to avoid the real issue, which is that training equals sacrifice. You *do* have to miss *Eastenders*.

By engaging in the daily battles of training and regular tests and trials, the mind and spirit get used to ignoring the pleading of our negative voices: the laziness, doubts and fears that bind us and keep us from doing what we really want to do.

Most of our barriers are of our own making. They are perceived rather than actual. That's why the world's most successful people are rarely the most talented; they are the most confident. Take a look at the pop charts if you need convincing.

They have self-belief and drive. They're not hindered by doubt.

It can be incredibly difficult to escape the traps and cages we set ourselves. Martial arts is one approach to working your way free. By engaging our fears, we dispel them. If they are a poison, we immunise ourselves by swallowing small, regular doses. Once our fears become familiar, they lose their hold over us.

Facing fear, with the help of an expert guide, is at the heart of the martial arts. The Sensei prepares his students for each test, tougher than the last, and pushes them through it so they can reap the rewards: deep-rooted self-belief. Freedom from fear.

Does it have to be done this way? I have come to believe it does. We can't rationalise our way out of fear. Confidence can't be acquired intellectually, because it doesn't belong in the head. It is forged in the heart, in the hottest flames, by raising dragons and slaying demons until there are none left to slay.

Epilogue

A year on, I'm still training, still assisting with the teaching at the club. I see my fellow students growing steadily under the outstanding instruction of our Sensei.

I see new students come and go. I see one or two that stay and knuckle down to the training. Then I watch them change before my eyes, from gawky kids with a bit of an attitude into strong fighters and excellent characters.

Each year at summer camp, a handful of students take their black belt grading. They put in a performance so outstanding that it would have been unthinkable even a year or two earlier. They are starting to become good teachers in their own right, helping newcomers with the basics of kata, bunkai or sparring, keeping the standards high, illuminating the path that we follow.

Since my own test, three more people have successfully completed the Thirty Man Kumite. Two were women, who I watched and cheered from the sidelines. One was a guy, who got a few friendly digs from me, right at the very end of his test.

Afterword

The martial arts have always claimed to deliver benefits over and above the practical and the physical. A great many people pay lip service to these holistic benefits. Yet when you look at most modern training regimes, it's difficult to see how these lessons might be gained. The Thirty Man Kumite is, without doubt, one event where they can.

On the surface, training to face 30 fighters, each one fresh, one after the other, in full-contact combat might be viewed as a purely physical endeavour. Indeed most, if not all, who set out on this incredible journey view it this way, at least at first. It's also true that some complete the task simply on a physical level. However, the greater benefits of this unique test are readily available to those who choose to fully accept the challenge and immerse themselves totally in the task.

Goran Powell is one such fighter and in this book, he has openly and skilfully articulated what others may have felt, but were unable to put into words.

Afterword

To witness courage is always a humbling experience. In writing this book, Goran again displays the courage he demonstrated on that day in 2002. It has taken courage to write this book because this is not the macho, chest-beating of a victorious fighter. This is the open, and at times painful, account of someone who pushed himself beyond anything he ever believed possible and emerged a better man – undoubtedly elevated as a martial artist, but at the same time humbled and awed by the experience.

Gavin Mulholland

Acknowledgements

I write for a living, but writing a book isn't the same as writing advertisements. It's a huge commitment and fraught with doubt. I'd never have finished the book without certain people who gave me the confidence to see it through.

The first was Geoff Thompson. I sent him a few chapters and asked him for advice. He rang the next day with words of encouragement and offered to write the foreword. I was incredibly moved by his support.

The second is my agent, Robin Wade, who offered advice and support when there was very little of it around. His belief in the book inspired me to complete it.

Thanks are also due to the following: my friend and teacher Gavin Mulholland, for his suggestions and insights; my father Michael for his help with the finer points of the English language; my fellow writers Julie Batsford-White and Peter Wise for their valuable input; my friend and colleague Adrian Nitsch for his striking front cover design and the highly-

Acknowledgements

regarded martial artist and writer Iain Abernethy, who helped me to get the book out there.

Finally, to my beautiful wife Charmaigne: thank you for your belief in me, your support in the difficult times and your love. Two years after I did the Thirty Man Kumite, Charmaigne did it too, and made a much better job of it than I did. But that's another story.

****

My thanks to the people from Daigaku Karate Kai named in this book. Clubs operate in London, Bristol and Torquay. If you'd like to find out more visit: www.goju-karate.co.uk

Education of a Martial Artist

If you want to study martial arts seriously, here are some books you may find useful. I haven't included technical manuals. You're better off finding these yourself for the art you're interested in.

These books will give you a deeper insight into aspects of all martial arts including strategy, fitness and philosophy. It's by no means a comprehensive list, so keep exploring. If you're not sure what to buy, go into a good bookshop rather than ordering off the net. You can read a few pages of the book itself, rather than being guided by the hype.

Martial Arts Classics

The Art of War
Sun Tzu

A classic text on combat strategy. The book covers advanced concepts simply and poetically. A must for any serious martial artist and, interestingly, it's often recommended for business studies too, where companies engage in 'marketing warfare'.

A Book of Five Rings
Miyamoto Mushashi

Another classic book of strategy by Japan's most famous swordsman. Enigmatic and deep, worth reading several times over the years as each reading reveals new depths.

On War
Von Clausewitz

A Western classic on warfare written by a Prussian soldier and still a foundation text for modern military study. A difficult read, though. The original was written in a rambling German style and then translated into English. The gems are there if you can force yourself to wade through the ore.

Hagekure – The Book of the Samurai
Yamamoto Tsunetomo

The classic Japanese text that sets out the harsh, Spartan lifestyle of the feudal Samurai. Not to be taken too literally today, but an interesting glimpse of the past that Japan still holds so dear.

Karate-do: My Way of Life
Gichin Funakoshi

Wonderful autobiography of the humble scholar and karate master who is widely credited with popularising karate in mainland Japan and hence the rest of the world. Funakoshi moved to Tokyo from his home on Okinawa and set up his famous Shotokan school.

The Kyokushin Way
Mas Oyama

A rare book containing the karate philosophy of Mas Oyama, one of the world's most famous masters and founder of the mighty Kyokushinkai. A valuable insight into the mindset of a legendary figure in the martial arts.

Bubishi: The Bible of Karate
Patrick McCarthy

The Bubishi was a classic text handed down from master to student in China and Okinawa detailing, among other things, vital points on the body. This translation by Patrick McCarthy also includes some karate history. The subject matter is too complex to be a 'how to' manual, but a fascinating read nonetheless. Mr McCarthy has researched traditional martial arts for many years in Japan, China and Okinawa and is himself a highly ranked master.

Fitness

Fighting Fit
David Mitchell

Good all-round book on martial arts fitness training, though there are plenty of similar books available nowadays, so shop around.

Fit to Fight
Peter Consterdine

A very motivating book full of great (and very painful) ideas for getting to the peak of fitness, including uphill sprints with a partner on your back.

Food for Sport
Jane Griffin

Good common-sense book about the right food and drink for anyone involved in hard physical exercise. Answers a lot of questions about what to eat and when.

Stretching Scientifically
Thomas Kurz

One of those rare books that completely changed the way I thought about a subject. Now widely accepted as one of the foremost reference books on stretching for martial artists, clearly written, scientifically proven, easy to follow and highly motivating. Buy it if you're getting nowhere with your flexibility.

Relax into Stretch
Pavel Tsatsouline

A short, simple book of stretching exercises written in an amusing manner, quite engaging, but make sure you read *Stretching Scientifically* for a more in-depth understanding of how it works.

244

Education of a Body Builder
Arnold Schwarzenegger

Love him or hate him, Arnold is never dull and his book is far more than a weight training manual. There's interesting background into the man and his will to succeed, plus tons of valuable observations about training and mental attitude. A great starting point for anyone who wants to improve their strength, both physical and mental.

Combat Conditioning
Matt Furey

I discovered this book by accident in a sports bookshop and found it amazingly useful and motivating. It contains simple, time-honoured wrestling exercises that have done wonders for my strength, especially my back and neck. (Start gently and build up because these are delicate areas and prone to injury.)

Boxing

If you're interested in how the world's most successful fighters think and feel, just pick up any boxing autobiography. You're probably in for a fascinating read. Once they hang up their gloves, most fighters have plenty of interesting tales to tell. They are usually down to earth and write quite openly and refreshingly about their lives, their successes and their failures.

When We Were Kings (Video/DVD)
Spike Lee

Wonderful award-winning documentary about the Rumble in the Jungle. Muhammad Ali breaks all the rules to beat the awesome George Foreman in one of the most thrilling upsets in boxing history.

The Tao of Muhammad Ali
Davis Miller

Muhammad Ali has become a cultural icon and there seems to be a new book about him every time I go into a bookshop! This one is by a karate practitioner who spent a lot of time with Ali and gives a good insight into the man behind the legend. There are plenty of other Ali books if you like this one.

Smokin' Joe: The Autobiography
Joe Frazier

After reading about Ali the legend, it's always useful to get a different perspective. Joe Frazier's views on things are understandably different to the general consensus, and adds some balance when Ali's halo begins to shine a little too brightly.

By George, The Autobiography of George Foreman
George Foreman

Another of Ali's famous opponents and now a preacher and TV personality, as famous today for his barbecue grill as for his thrilling fights in the seventies and his amazing comeback to the boxing ring in later life.

Corner Men: Great Boxing Trainers
Ronald K. Fried

If you want to know how the world's greatest boxers got to be so good, look at their trainers. This book reveals the ideas of some of the world's best-known trainers, plus some fascinating insight into how different boxers need different methods to get to the top.

In the Corner
Dave Anderson

I'm often surprised how little boxing training has changed over the years. Today's top fighters still use training methods similar to those used in the early part of last century. I guess the human body and the pugilistic arts have been understood at a high level for a long time.

George Francis: Trainer of Champions
George Francis

Another revealing book by the man who's spent a lifetime training young men to become fighters, most notably Frank Bruno and John Conteh.

Dark Trade
Donald McRae

Thought provoking look at the character and motivation of some of the world's top fighters, and explores some of the unpalatable truths about the so called 'noble art'.

War, Baby: The Glamour of Violence
Kevin Mitchell

This book is about one of the most ferocious fights ever seen: Nigel Benn v Gerald McClellan. The fight left McClellan fighting for his life. Like *Dark Trade* (above) it raises some difficult questions for fight fans about the sport they enjoy so much.

The Soul of Boxing
Phil Shirley

This book is about various top boxers. There's a great bit from Evander Holyfield about his mindset before his first fight with Mike Tyson, which he won, against the odds.

Eastern Philosophy

The link between religion and the martial arts is well-known, but remember that Eastern systems such as Buddhism, Taoism and Zen differ considerably from Christianity. I'm simplifying greatly, but they don't have a 'God' as such. They concentrate on reaching a perfect state of harmony with the world around us. They might just as easily be described as forms of spiritualism or philosophy instead of religion, though they contain elements of all three.

The systematic study of martial arts is widely accepted as beginning in the Shaolin Temple in China in the sixth century. The Buddhist monk Bodhidarma came to Shaolin from India and founded Ch'an Buddhism, which became 'Zen' when it reached Japan. Bodhidarma taught the monks exercises to help them with the rigours of meditation and this physical training later developed into martial arts.

Taoism is a Chinese system concerned with health, longevity and living in a natural way. It is integral to the so called 'internal' Chinese martial arts, notably Tai Chi.

Buddhism Plain and Simple
Steve Hagan

Brilliant in its clarity and deeply inspiring. If you want to get your head around what Buddhism and Zen is all about, read this. Hagan makes perfect sense of a complicated subject and his book will help you appreciate the beauty of Buddhist thought like no other.

Bodhidarma
Red Pine

Short and enigmatic translation of writings thought to have been the philosophy of Bodhidarma, the father of Zen and Kung Fu.

Art of Just Sitting
John Daido Loori

If you've ever sat in meditation before or after a martial arts class and wondered what you should be thinking about, this is the book for you. Clearly written and not too hard to understand.

Zen Flesh, Zen Bones
Nyogen Senzaki

A collection of stories, parables and *koans* (Zen riddles) and a good all round introduction to the mysteries of Zen.

Tao Te Ching
Lau Tzu

A great starting point on Taoism, short, poetic, enigmatic and beautifully written, worth re-reading every so often to see how much more you can understand.

A Taoist Classic
Chuang Tsu

Another useful text to expand your knowledge of the mysterious Tao.

Western Philosophy

If you want to get really interesting, try some Western philosophy and look for parallels. You'll discover plenty of similar ideas that are simply expressed differently due to natural differences in language and culture.

History of Western Philosophy
Bertrand Russell

The ultimate 'beginner's guide' to Western philosophy. Russell is a prominent philosopher himself and his book covers all the great Western thinkers from the ancient Greeks to the present day. If you liked *The Matrix*, check the chapter on Descartes and his question on reality: is it all an illusion created by an evil demon?

Republic
Plato

I wasn't expecting to understand very much of this book, so I was delighted when I found that I could. It's written in a simple, straightforward style that makes it an enlightening read. Some of Plato's most famous ideas are clearly expressed, like what makes a horse a horse, and the shadows in the cave.

The Monk and the Philosopher
Jean-Francois Revel, Matthieu Ricard

A fascinating book that explores the parallels between Eastern and Western thought. It takes the form of a conversation between a father who is a Western professor of philosophy and his son, who is a Buddhist monk living in Tibet.

The Barefoot Doctor's Handbook for the Urban Warrior: A Spiritual Guide
Stephen Russell

A light-hearted look at how the ancient knowledge of the Taoists can help us now in the daily rat race. A very easy read (which can be welcome if you're tired of reading countless books about mind, body and spirit that leave you totally confused). Full of good sense too.

Tibetan Book of the Dead / Tibetan Book of Living and Dying
Various translations

The *Tibetan Book of the Dead* is a classic Buddhist text about understanding and coping with death. I must confess I found the writing hard work. There are various translations on the market now, so perhaps another version might be easier to follow. The *Tibetan Book of Living and Dying* appears to be a modern adaptation of the same ideas and it's easier to understand.

General

Watch My Back
Geoff Thompson

Geoff's brutally honest book on martial arts, door work and his personal battles to get himself to where he really wanted to be, and now belongs. A thrilling read and a real eye-opener for any serious martial artist. Highly recommended.

Fear, the Friend of Extraordinary People
Geoff Thompson

Just around the time I was beginning to formulate my own rather simple theories on fear, and how to cope with it (you can't avoid it) I came across this book which explained it all one easy read. Geoff combines scientific explanations about the effects of adrenaline with psychology and good old-fashioned experience. It's reassuring to know that this book was not written by an academic in an ivory tower, but by someone who has regularly faced violence as part of his former job.

Bunkai Jutsu
Iain Abernethy

This is a great book if you have been practising kata without knowing why, or you've been shown some 'moves' that are very unconvincing. Iain unravels the mysteries better than anyone I've come across in print, with simple, realistic explanations and a profound understanding of the strategy and principles contained in kata. His videos are excellent too.

About the Author

Goran Powell was born in Worcester in 1965. He joined his local judo club at the age of seven and trained in the martial arts ever since. Today he holds the rank of fourth dan black belt in Goju Ryu karate. He works as a freelance writer in advertising and is a regular contributor to the martial arts press. Goran has two children, Harry and Hannah, and lives in London with his wife Charmaigne.